From the files of THE NATIONAL ENQUIRER

DRIVEN TO KILL

THE CLARA HARRIS STORY

BY **CLIFF LINEDECKER**

Edited by Nicholas Maier

American Media, Inc.

DRIVEN TO KILL
The Clara Harris Story

Copyright © 2003 AMI Books, Inc.

Cover design: Carlos Plaza
Interior design: Debbie Browning

ISBN: 1-932270-11-6

First printing: August 2003

Printed in the United States of America

10 9 8 7 6 5 4 3 2 1

INTRODUCTION

The upscale suburbs of Friendswood, League City, Clear Lake and Nassau Bay were yuppie heaven. Clustered around schools, churches, and sparkling new shopping malls, the quiet neighborhoods filled with custom-built homes seemed to offer all of the good things in life. Reaching outward from the Johnson Space Center and Houston's southern edge, this was an area where soccer moms delivered their kids in SUVs to classes and after-school activities ranging from cheerleading practice and ballet lessons to Little League and Boy and Girl Scout meetings. These prosperous suburbs, like so many scattered around cities throughout the country, appeared to be the last place in the world where the serenely comfortable lives of the residents would be spoiled by murder.

Curiously, perhaps, because it occurs so often, murder is one of society's most sacrosanct taboos. Literature's most brilliant authors and playwrights have crafted books and plays pointing to the certain retribution for violating the proscription against taking the life of another. The Bible and other religious writings strongly condemn murder and warn of certain and terrible punishment for violators.

"If he smite him ... so that he die, he is a murderer; the murderer shall surely be put to death," the Old Testament warns in Numbers XXXV, 16. The great taboo is also mentioned in Matthew, XIX, which declares: "Jesus said, Thou shalt do no murder."

But despite all the repeated warnings and the universal horror created by the act, murder has been with mankind since Cain killed Abel.

Each year in the United States, about 25,000 people are fatally shot, stabbed, strangled, bludgeoned and murdered in various other ways. And like the biblical Cain, killers are most often men. Testosterone-driven males with their naturally aggressive and competitive instincts who take the lives of other human beings are a dime a dozen. Serial killers vie with each other to see who can rack up the most notches on their guns, snuffing out male and female prostitutes, hitchhikers, barroom pickups, unwary college coeds and delicately frail old women — sometimes for no reason at all except for the rush of excitement and the unique feeling of power.

Women are more often victims, survivors or observers rather than perpetrators. They are expected to love and nurture and to create life, not take it. When women do cross the line, a disproportionate number kill a member of their family or someone else with close emotional attachments such as a former mate or boyfriend. When a woman sees a treasured relationship suddenly crumbling around her feet because a husband has left her for another, she can become a vengeful harpy with murder on her mind.

Clara Harris was an exceptional woman and about the closest thing to the perfect wife and mother that anyone could have expected. She was devoted to her family and to her church.

Then, on one terrible midsummer night, her emotions spilled over. She suddenly snapped, lashing out with all the lethal fury of a West Texas tornado at the man who had done her wrong. By the time the smoke began to settle, the wreckage of a modern-day Greek tragedy had been left in the South Houston suburbs of East Texas — and no one was left unscathed.

CHAPTER 1

"David, look what you made me do!"

Shortly before 9 p.m.
Wednesday, July 24, 2002

Oscar Torres, Chris Junco and Ashok Moza were lobbing tennis balls on separate courts across from the back parking lot of the posh Nassau Bay Hilton Inn when suddenly they heard the roar of a powerful engine and the shrill screech of tires. They and other witnesses watched in horror and stunned disbelief as a silver Mercedes-Benz S-class sedan roared out of the evening darkness and across the lighted parking lot, sliced into the driver-side door of a parked Lincoln Navigator and slammed into a man helping a woman into the front seat.

Seconds before veering into the black sports utility vehicle, the Mercedes brushed 24-year-old hotel employee Paul Garrett Clark. Unhurt but shaken by the narrow escape, the front desk clerk glanced at the man holding open the door of the parked car and saw his eyes bulge in terror a moment before the Mercedes plowed into him.

Peering toward the hotel from the tennis courts, Moza at first thought the heavy object that vaulted onto the hood of the 4,000 pound luxury sedan and dropped moistly to the pavement was a duffel bag. Then the Baytown resident realized that the crumpled object sprawled on the hard-paved surface of the parking lot was the broken body of a man.

The tennis players watched in horror as a screaming teenage girl opened the passenger side door of the Mercedes and touched her feet on the pavement as if she was trying to stop the car or get out. She lurched back into her seat when the driver of the Mercedes gunned the engine and began circling a grassy median strip, coming back around for another pass.

The heavy car was driven around the circle and rolled over the victim at least three times, according to some witnesses.

Watching the grisly scene, 35-year-old Junco later recalled in court testimony that it was hard to believe the events he was watching were really happening. "It was weird. I don't know how to describe it," he said. "I even thought the car was pissed off at him."

After bumping over the man for the last time, the Mercedes lurched to a stop next to his body. The teenager scrambled out the passenger side door, screaming, "My dad, my dad, you killed my dad." The girl punched the driver in the face with her fist and then collapsed onto the pavement, sobbing uncontrollably.

The driver, a beautiful and well-dressed middle-age woman, appeared stunned and stood by the car for a few moments as if she was confused and wasn't quite sure what she was doing there or what was going on. Then she stumbled to the broken body of the man sprawled in a widening pool of blood on the concrete pavement and knelt beside him. He was bleeding from his nose and mouth, and struggling for breath. "Oh, David. Oh, David," the woman wailed. "Oh, my God, what have I done?"

Kneeling in the blood she pleaded, "Are you

OK? Don't leave me." Placing a hand on his chest, she desperately sought to detect a heartbeat and then began feeling for a pulse. As bystanders rushed to the scene to help, she cupped his face in her hands and cried, "David, look what you made me do!"

Julie Creger and her fiancé, Robert Williams, a diesel technician from Conroe, Texas, were vacationing with her children and relaxing at the hotel's outdoor waterfront pool facing the placid waters of nearby Clear Lake when they heard the commotion and ran to the scene. Creger pushed the driver away and took her place beside the victim. He was a bloody mess, making gurgling sounds and gasping for air.

Trained in CPR to care for a premature son, Creger knew she had to open an airway in the man's throat so he could breathe and she had to do it quickly. The woman tried to pry open his tightly clenched jaw, but it was broken and she couldn't force it apart. His teeth were jarred loose by the impact with the car and the pavement, so she pushed a finger into his mouth in an effort to open an airway and get him breathing again. A bloody tooth fell out into her hand and she placed it on the ground.

Creger knew she was rapidly losing the battle to keep this man alive and his desperate gasps were increasingly labored. His breath was moist and his chest congested as he drowned in his own blood. Then she noticed his right ear, mangled and nearly sheared off by the impact. Creger used a towel she carried with her from the pool to wipe his face and sop up some of the blood pooling around him.

"I realized there was no more help I could give him at that point, because I couldn't get his jaw unclenched," the woman later testified in court. So she held his hand and talked to him, urging him to keep breathing and attempting to assure him that everything was going to be OK.

While she was doing her best to help the injured man, her fiancé joined the teenager and the victim's female companion who were standing next to the damaged SUV. The older woman had injuries of her own and appeared stunned by the pain and violence. The girl sobbed that her name was Lindsey. Struggling to talk through the tears, the teenager said that the bloodied man was her father.

Creger turned her attention to helping the girl, who was hyperventilating, as Williams took over at the side of the injured man. Lindsey asked if her father was dead.

Walking her away from the body, Creger asked, "Lindsey, who did this?"

"My mom, I mean my stepmom," she choked out in reply.

"Sweetie, did she mean to do this?"

"Yes," the girl gasped.

Williams realized just how badly maimed the victim was when he ran his hands lightly over David's body to check his injuries. The mechanic couldn't detect any ribs on his lower right side and couldn't feel his right lung expand. On the left side, it felt like two or three ribs were missing and his lung was expanding only about half of its normal capacity.

"David, look at me. Breathe, breathe," Williams pleaded. He didn't want the man to die in front of the teenager. When there was no response, Williams gently thumped the horribly maimed victim on the chin and told him, "Your daughter is watching you, you need to breathe."

The efforts of Williams and his fiancée to save the life of the injured man were fruitless.

—————

It was the next day before the Good Samaritans and other witnesses learned the full identity of the major performers in the Shakespearean-like tragedy that played out in the brightly lighted parking lot.

The dead man was David Lynn Harris, a 44-year-old orthodontist who had offices in Clear Lake, a short distance from the hotel. The driver of the Mercedes was his wife, Clara Suarez Harris, also 44 and a dentist, and his partner in a chain of busy dental clinics in Clear Lake and other nearby Houston suburbs. The petite woman David Harris was helping into the parked black Navigator when he was rammed and run over was his mistress and office receptionist, Gail Bridges.

CHAPTER 2

A marriage made in heaven

L ooking back on the marriage of her youngest son and daughter-in-law 10 years after their wedding in 1992, Mildred Harris described the union as "a marriage made in heaven."

The families attended the same church, Shadycrest Baptist, and the two women were so fond of each other that they socialized and chatted together more like best friends than mother-in-law and daughter-in-law. It all seemed perfectly natural, because they were brought together by their mutual love for David Lynn Harris, Mildred's son and Clara's husband. Clara was firmly convinced that she and David were perfectly suited for each other, in part because they had learned and matured after each of them experienced a previous unsuccessful marriage.

The Colombian-born beauty told a local newspaper, *The Brazosport Facts*, which ran a story about her dental practice, that her mother advised her years earlier that "American men were wonderful."

"She was right," Clara proudly beamed. "I found the best. I found the one God had reserved for me."

David was easy to like and to love. His employees at Space Center Orthodontics in Clear Lake were fond of their boss and admired him for his professional skills, hard work ethic and devotion to his wife. He wasn't the type who came into the office late and hung over because he had been out half of the night with a bunch of buddies at a sports bar guzzling beer, watching the Houston Rockets on television.

Even after David bought an expensive toupee to cover his rapidly receding hairline and

expanding bald spot, he didn't chase other
women or flirt with any of his more attractive
patients. His office manner was totally professional and the woman he was married to was
the center of his life. He boasted to family
members and friends about how loving and
creative Clara was. David had good reason to be
proud, because his wife was not only intelligent,
industrious and an excellent businesswoman,
but she was also a beauty.

Born in Bogota as an only child, Clara grew
up with a healthy respect for hard work and a
determination to support herself and help care
for her mother. She was only 6 years old when
her father, an electrical engineer, died and left
her mother a widow.

After practicing dentistry in Colombia, Clara
moved to the United States in the late 1980s for
more training and signed up for classes at
Washington University in St. Louis. After earning her degree in dentistry in 1990, she was
accepted for a graduate program with the dental
branch of the University of Texas Health Science
Center in Houston. She served her residency at
the nearby Memorial Hermann Hospital.

One of the first friends she made after inter-
viewing at UT was Shelly Canada, who was
already a dental resident. Years later Canada

recalled that she "fell instantly in love with this beautiful woman that was everything you could want in a friend." Clara was like that; when she made friends, they were friends for life.

The friendship between the two dental professionals would last through good times and bad. While Canada forged a successful career that included service as president of a local dental association, Clara married the man of her dreams, constructed her own rapidly expanding business, then watched her dazzling Cinderella life turn into a ghastly nightmare.

But everything was still turning up roses for the long-legged brunette with the beauty mark mole on her left cheek when she was selected as Miss Colombia Houston shortly after completing her residency at Memorial Hermann.

David was no slacker either and he grew up with a similarly strong work ethic and desire to succeed. The son of Gerald and Mildred Harris, he was the youngest child of a family that included three older siblings. His father was a high school principal in Pearland, a heavily working class suburb of Houston with a large minority population. The elder Harris later headed the district transportation department. David graduated from high school in Pearland after piling up an impressive academic record and participating in extracurricular activities that included membership in the marching band.

He studied dentistry at Indiana University in Bloomington, Indiana, majoring in orthodontics. In September 1990 after beginning his final year at IU, he and his first wife separated and she filed for divorce the following month. According to the divorce records, "Certain disputes and differences have arisen and have existed for some time in the past between husband and wife, and as a result of said differences, they separated." David and the former Debra S. Turner were married five years when their divorce was finalized in July 1991.

Court records also note that the couple reached an amicable settlement and understanding. As part of that understanding, it was agreed that Debra would "exchange the VCR for the loveseat in husband's possession prior to his relocation to Texas."

The former Mrs. David Harris was also given custody of the couple's daughter, Lindsey Nicole. David agreed to carry a life insurance policy for no less than $50,000, listing the girl as beneficiary. He was awarded summer visitation and half of the Christmas vacation with his daughter, and agreed to pay her travel expenses. David was also ordered to pay $550 monthly in child support. Additionally, the agreement called for David to pay for Lindsey's fees and tuition at a state-supported college or its equivalent, her room and board and books.

After returning home in 1991 with his VCR and a Master's of Science degree from IU, he continued his study of orthodontics at the Houston Dental Branch of the University of Texas Health Science Center. He graduated second in his class and quickly began showing a business sense that equaled his skill in his dental specialty.

Like his parents, David was strongly committed to the Christian faith and dutifully attended devotional services at Shadycrest Baptist Church in Pearland. He played drums there with the Colemans, a Christian soft-rock group. He kept in good physical shape by waterskiing, swimming and boating on local freshwater lakes or off the beaches on nearby Galveston Bay.

According to some reports, Clara and David met while they were students at UT, but other accounts indicate they first met while working at the Castle Dental Center in Houston. A Castle spokesman later said they had no record of either Clara or David working there.

Regardless of which account is true, soon after meeting for the first time the two young dentists were head-over-heels in love.

David described the charming woman he was
in love with to his parents and friends in glow-
ing terms. They dated less than a year before
tying the knot, and true to her romantic nature,
Clara Leonor Suarez selected Valentine's Day as
the day she would become Mrs. David Harris.

The couple hosted their wedding reception at
the Nassau Bay Hilton Inn, which was just
across the road from the internationally known
space center that was home to NASA's mission
control and the astronaut corps. The upper
floors of the luxurious hotel provided breath-
taking views of the space center and of the placid
waters of Clear Lake and its 83-slip marina.

A year later, Clara had already bought her own
dental practice in Lake Jackson, Brazoria
County, and they were living in David's hometown of Pearland when he was fired from his job.
She supported both of them until he established
his own practice, Space Center Orthodontics, in
a strip shopping mall in Clear Lake.

Selecting a business name linked to the space
center only a few miles away wasn't unique for
either Houston or for the southern suburbs.
Many other businesses took advantage of the
name recognition of the huge operational and
training complex by linking it to everything
from pizza parlors and submarine sandwich

shops to barbershops and saloons. Even Houston's professional baseball team was named the Astros and the Aeros represented the city in the International Hockey League.

Years after the Harris wedding, former Pearland neighbors recalled the couple as being totally enamored with each other. They weren't like some couples who walked into social gatherings, then barely saw each other again until it was time to leave. David and Clara stood together, danced together and chatted with friends together.

The couple also made a good team professionally. She specialized in pediatric dentistry and he drove to her clinic, Lake Jackson Dental Care, a couple of days a week to provide orthodontic services for her patients. A colleague later described them as running their business like "a one-stop shop." Clara treated children for general dentistry, then passed them along to her husband when they needed braces and other orthodontic care. Everything was kept in the family.

The high-energy couple began developing their own chain of dental clinics. Most were concentrated around the upscale suburban areas south of Houston, especially in towns and malls near the bustling space center. When the couple set up their corporation, Clara was named as the majority owner with 51 percent of the stock. As the business grew and more dental clinics were added, David took on most of the responsibility for staffing and setting up a management team.

By 2001 he was clearing $35,000 in an average month just at Space Center Orthodontics and combined with Clara's earnings and their rapidly growing chain of dental clinics, the Harris family income was heading for the stratosphere. They owned a house about 80 miles north of Houston on Lake Livingston, which was one of the largest and most scenic bodies of water in Texas. They also had property in Colorado.

For a time it appeared that the only thing interfering with their idyllic life together was Clara's difficulty becoming pregnant. Although David's daughter, Lindsey, who lived with her mother and stepfather in Columbus, Ohio, was a frequent visitor, the couple wanted children of their own. When Clara still hadn't become pregnant after five years of marriage, David proposed they seek help at a clinic and begin fertility treatments. In September 1998 the delighted couple became parents of twin boys, Brian David Harris and Bradley Evan Harris.

Family and friends, including members of

their church, were overjoyed. The Reverend Stephen M. Daily, the Shadycrest Baptist pastor, was present with David at the Women's Hospital of Texas when the twins were born. He prayed that God would fill the family's life with love and blessings.

With the birth of the boys it seemed that the onetime Bogota girl had it all — a doting husband, healthy twin sons and a job she loved. She was living the American dream with her family in a magnificent white stone and brick home worth more than a half-million dollars, custom built on a spacious four-acre corner lot with a long, circular driveway at the front entrance.

The Harris mansion was in the Polly Ranch Estates section of a larger bedroom community named Friendswood, a suburb filled with young families of upscale professionals much like their own. Neighbors got used to seeing Clara's mother pushing the boys in a stroller up and down Pine Drive. There was even a Spanish-speaking nanny for the boys. By 2001, when Clara bought herself a slightly used but prized $70,000 silver Mercedes-Benz S-class sedan, it was merely the icing on the cake.

As busy as she was with her personal dental practice and the expansion of the family business, Clara chatted by phone with her husband two or three times a day, always making sure to remind him that she loved him. She kept photos of him and the boys in her office and conscientiously updated them every month. She also made certain that she finished with her patients in time to get home and cook dinner for the family.

But Clara was spreading herself dangerously thin while keeping up her role as a pediatric dentist, businesswoman, wife and mother to two demanding toddlers. She may not have realized that was creating a dangerous situation, because her middle-age husband had grown used to being the center of her world.

CHAPTER 3

Gail

Some divorces, the lucky ones, are relatively painless. Others, especially when kids are involved, can get downright nasty.

Gail Bridges' breakup with her husband, Steven Bridges, was one of the nasty ones. And it seemed to get nastier almost by the day as the couple fought over their personal differences and over their three kids. Gail's close friendship with a female chum who was undergoing her own divorce woes and amateur detective work by both husbands, played major roles in the rapid degeneration of her 10-year marriage.

Before the breakup, Gail and Steven Bridges seemed to be living the good life in the comfortable Houston suburbs, like their friends, Charles "Chuck" and Julie Ann Knight, another glittering up-and-coming League City couple with kids. A husky 5-foot-8-inch tall blue-eyed blond, Chuck was a software specialist for an aerospace company. Julie, also a blue-eyed blonde, was a full-time mother and homemaker.

The Bridges and Knights were close and got together to dine out, to celebrate New Year's Eve, the kids' birthdays and other special occasions. Gail and Julie took tennis lessons together, worked out with each other at the gym and regularly met for outings at local shopping malls. The families even attended the same church, Bay Harbor United Methodist.

Belinda Gail Thompson grew up as the daughter of Oliver Thompson, a deacon in the First Baptist Church, and church had always been an important part of her life. Hardly anyone called her "Belinda," and she was known to most of her friends and acquaintances by her middle name, "Gail." She spent her childhood in the flyspeck town of Crosby a few miles northeast of Houston — one of those communities that is easy to miss if you blink your eyes while driving through.

Gail was one of the most popular girls at Crosby High School. Bright, inquisitive and energetic, she was a cheerleader for three years. She also performed in the marching band, served on the student council, on the yearbook staff her senior year, belonged to the Medical Career Club, to the Audubon club and participated in speech and poetry activities.

Her father served for a time on the local school board, so she kept her grades up and after graduation in 1981, enrolled at Lee College in Baytown on Galveston Bay where she earned an associate's degree. She continued her education at the University of Southwest Louisiana in Lafayette, La., and at the University of Houston.

Gail and Steve tied the knot on July 16, 1988, and from all appearances they were a classic all-American couple.

Steve Bridges was a button-down type of man, always dressing neatly in a suit and tie before leaving for his job as a State Farm Insurance agent. Gail also liked to dress up and was often seen wearing a crisply pressed frock or fashionable pantsuit, but her wardrobe also included a fine assortment of party dresses. Her jewelry included a diamond wedding ring, Rolex watch and several gold necklaces. Steve was proud of his pretty wife, could afford to indulge her and he did exactly that.

The young couple was living the good life and, shortly before the marriage began to sour, they bought matching Lincoln Navigators. Hers was fire engine red and his was white. An acquaintance recalled years later that Steve treated his wife like a princess. She wasn't a former beauty queen like Clara Harris, but she was petite and provocative, with snowy white skin that was shown off to perfection by lustrous dark hair and expressive almond-brown eyes.

Although the family genes had been good to her, she gave nature a helping hand by prettying up her pixie frame with breast implants. The young homemaker was so proud of her new profile that she eagerly shared her secret with friends and even with people she knew only slightly. She was quick to advise other women on the benefits of breast enlargement, an acquaintance later recalled.

Steve Bridges was a good salesman and found success in the insurance business. High-paying jobs with high incomes were all over the place and available for both blue- and white-collar workers with education and skills that could be put to use with NASA, the booming petroleum industry and a host of subsidiary employers. Businesses were expanding, causing huge shopping malls, schools, churches and homes to pop up like mushrooms all over the South Houston suburbs. The highways and the streets in the burgeoning communities were filled with sparkling new SUVs, shiny pickup trucks, convertibles and sports cars. Everyone needed insurance of one kind or another.

Steve did a booming business that produced sufficient income for the growing family to move into the exclusive gated community of South Shore Harbor in League City, part of the widening sprawl of old and new communities between Houston, Texas City and Galveston. It also bordered Friendswood to the south and east.

In the early years of the Bridges' marriage, the young couple attended St. Mary's Catholic Church and the older children attended the church school. When the family left St. Mary's and joined the Bay Harbor United Methodist Church, the kids transferred to the Ferguson Elementary School in their own neighborhood.

Gail seemed the typical suburban mom, driving her kids to school, soccer practice or church activities, then joining other young mothers for coffee in one of the local malls, or having her Dorothy Hamill haircut trimmed and freshened up at a salon. At other times she would slip on a pair of hip-hugging jeans and a top, then climb into her pride-and-joy Lincoln Navigator and pick up her best friend, Julie Knight, so they could spend an idle afternoon together.

The perky, raven-haired Gail and her curvaceous blond friend spent so much time together that it seemed almost as if they were joined at the hip. At least once they took off on a vacation just for the two of them at the Knights' condominium in Colorado. Gail even recuperated from her breast implant surgery at Julie's home, according to an acquaintance.

It would be this intimate relationship that caused their fairy-tale lives to begin turning sour in late 1998. By 1999 both marriages were in serious trouble. Their husbands had begun to suspect they were having a lesbian affair.

In January, unknown to the women, Julie's husband, Chuck, telephoned a private detective agency called Blue Moon Investigations in the nearby town of Webster and asked to have his wife and her girlfriend shadowed to confirm his suspicions that they were involved in a lesbian relationship. He talked with the agency's vice president, Bobbi Bacha, who did much of the investigating.

When she was queried later about the conversation, Bobbi said the client told her that he and Steve Bridges were splitting the cost. When he was later asked about the incident, Chuck denied he ever said anything about sharing the fee.

Blue Moon Investigations took on the job and Chuck put the bill for the surveillance, $55-an-hour for a four-hour minimum, on his credit card. According to Bobbi, he explained that he and Steve Bridges had arranged to baby-sit with the kids so their wives could get away for a couple of hours of girl talk and shopping at the Baybrook Mall. The arrangement would provide a good opportunity for the sleuths from Blue Moon to follow the women around and see what they were really up to.

Chuck made it clear that he didn't think the girls-night-out shopping trip was as innocent as it was cracked up to be, according to scribbled notes Bobbi later shared with a writer for *Texas Monthly* magazine.

"I bet they will go to a hotel. Or they might just pull over on the side of a highway to do their business," he reportedly confided. "Gail has a boob job and my wife will not be able to wait to touch those puppies." Later, Chuck would deny that he referred to Gail's breasts as "puppies."

Chuck reportedly confided to the investigator that he disabled Julie's car to make it easier for the wives to be tailed, explaining that Gail drove slower than Julie and her SUV was bright red and easier to keep track of.

Bobbi drove to the Harbor Park subdivision in League City where she waited for Gail and Julie to leave the Knight house. Julie bounded out of the house wearing blue jeans and a bright red designer top. Gail also wore jeans and had pulled on a pink top.

The Blue Moon gumshoe followed the women as they drove off in the red Navigator and then stopped at the mall. She watched while they checked out a few stores, then chatted and tried on shoes at Nine West. Bobbi settled into a seat nearby and fussed with a pair of stiletto heels, keeping an eye on Gail and Julie the entire time. And she trailed unobtrusively along when they left and drove to a McDonald's, where they ordered a couple of soft drinks before going home.

Bobbi reported to Chuck the next day that she had observed nothing about the women's behavior to indicate there was something romantic or sexual about their relationship. Their heads were close together as they rode in the Navigator, but that was perfectly natural if they were talking, as they appeared to be. Bobbi asked Chuck if he knew women were different than men and it wasn't unusual for them to hug and kiss.

Forced to recall the surveillance a few years later, Bobbi compared the two chums to animated characters from the popular television cartoon, *The Flintstones*. "They were like Wilma and Betty," she said. "They shopped together, had their kids together. They were friends."

Bobbi Bacha and Blue Moon didn't work for Chuck Knight again. But it wouldn't be long before she and her agency were back smack-dab in the middle of the rapidly mushrooming marital free-for-all that was developing around the Knights and the Bridges.

The young housewives filed for divorce in the spring of 1999 — Julie on April 22 and Gail six days later on April 28. Gail cited discord and personality conflicts as grounds for dissolving her decade-long marriage. In a countersuit, Steve accused his wife of cruel treatment and claimed she was having a romantic affair with Julie.

Shortly after that, Gail and Julie showed up at the second floor offices of Blue Moon in the Morgan Stanley building on Bay Area Boulevard, unaware this was the very agency that had been commissioned to tail them only months before. Over steaming cups of herbal tea, the women told Bobbi they were worried their husbands were planning to accuse them in court papers of being lesbians as part of a maneuver to force them to agree to out-of-court settlements that would short-change them in their property settlements. Stories were circulating around town that they were more than just "friends" and they thought their husbands were behind the embarrassing development.

The two chums confided that they suspected their husbands were trying to entrap them and sometimes telephoned to tell them to "get naked in bed together and we'll be there later," Bobbi eventually told the *Houston Chronicle*.

"Some women will do a lot of things to please their husbands, but, thank God, they didn't," the experienced private eye sagely observed. "It's sad because they are very good mothers. They take their children very seriously."

But what really brought the women to Blue Moon was that Julie suspected her husband of being involved in an affair and wanted the agency to shadow him. Gail didn't want to stir up passions over her messy divorce any more than they already were and decided against putting a similar tail on Steve.

Bobbi assigned one of her investigators to tail Chuck and within a few days she had developed a startling report for Julie. Gail trailed along with her friend to hear the news. The detective agency chief reported that her investigator observed Chuck visiting the house of a friend near his home and that a woman was also showing up there at about the same time. Soon after that, the investigator caught Chuck and the woman flying to Tampa, Florida, for a weekend getaway, she said.

When confronted with the accusation, Chuck admitted he was seeing someone, but claimed he only began dating again after he and Julie separated.

But the biggest surprise came when Bobbi identified the woman involved in the back-alley affair. It was Laurie Wells, a part-time baton-twirling instructor who was one of Julie and Gail's closest friends. She and her contractor husband, Steve, lived in Dickinson, one of the smaller communities in the scatter of suburbs sprinkled between Houston and Galveston. The town adjoined League City on the south.

Gail first met Laurie at a Lamaze class and invited her to attend Bay Harbor Methodist. The Wells couple then began socializing with the Bridges and the Knights.

Shortly after Bobbi Bacha revealed her startling report, the Wells broke up, contributing to the marital fireworks that were exploding inside and outside the family courts in nearby Galveston. Wedding pictures, dresses, tools and pieces of perfectly good furniture were turning up in the trash all over the suburbs. It seemed almost as if divorce was a deadly germ or bacteria — and the infection was spreading.

Three couples who once socialized together, attended the same church and drove their kids back and forth to school events were spitting and scratching like a nest of feral cats stuffed together into a sack. Nerves were frazzled and sensitivities rubbed so raw that it didn't take much to spark full-scale confrontations.

The divorce files at the Galveston County Courthouse were soon bulging with allegations of threatening messages left on voice mail, stalking, harassment, middle-finger salutes and shouting matches at the mall while embarrassed shoppers and clerks stared — or pretended not to notice. Julie claimed Chuck followed her in his car and all three of the battling couples bickered in and out of court over the kids and division of their joint property.

With all the sensational stories of lesbian high jinks, bed-hopping, stalking and spying among the yuppie couples making the rounds, Houston's southern suburbs were beginning to look like a sleazy combination of *Peyton Place* and *The Osbournes*. Some people sarcastically snickered that was why suburbs are so often referred to as "bedroom communities."

Julie hired attorney Valerie W. Davenport, who also assisted Gail in her court proceedings. The Houston lawyer accused both husbands of manufacturing the accusations of lesbianism to cover up their own misconduct. She also claimed in court documents that Steve abused alcohol and prescription pills. Both husbands denied all of the accusations.

When Gail was asked during the divorce proceedings if she ever had sexual contact with Julie, she replied that the question was "overly broad and vague."

And when she was asked if she had ever had intercourse or "other sexual contact" with anyone other than her husband since her marriage, she gave a similar response. The term "other sexual contact" was too broad and vague, she said.

But she replied with a firm, "No," when she was asked if she had indulged in sexual intercourse with anyone besides her husband.

The prolonged divorce proceedings and bitter skirmishing was devastating, especially for the children. In late 2000 Steven and Gail were parents of a 5-year-old boy, a 10-year-old boy and an 8-year-old girl. The Knights had a 10-year-old daughter and a 6-year-old son. Steve and Laurie Wells had two girls, who were 7 and 9 in 1999.

The kids were caught in the middle by the catastrophic family upheavals. They not only had to deal with their parents being constantly at each other's throats, but some of them had to put up with schoolyard whispers and rumors about the sexuality of their mothers. While the battle raged, the children were pulled and twisted in a wrenching tug-of-war between their feuding parents.

The Bridges' divorce became final in December 1999 and the Knights followed close behind, making it official the following January. The court named Gail and Steve as joint managing conservators of their children, meaning they would share custody. The two youngest children lived with Gail and the oldest boy stayed with his father. Julie kept her two children, who by that time were 11 and 7 years old, but she and Chuck were also named as joint managing conservators.

Laurie Wells lost out in the battle over her kids. Her ex-husband was given custody of the girls, reportedly in part because he taped a phone call from her threatening to teach them to hate him — then played it in court.

Despite the finalization of their divorce, the feud between the former Knight family husband and wife continued to simmer and smoke, with fitful bouts of back-and-forth sniping. Julie returned to court seeking protective orders against Chuck, whom she accused of stalking and harassing her and the kids.

Chuck stayed in the family home in the Harbor Park subdivision when he and Julie separated and she moved into an apartment in the Clear Lake area. Gail lived just across the street.

By the spring of 2001 the women purchased their own homes. Gail moved into a two-story brown brick home on Lake Lodge in the Bay Forest subdivision in May. In June Julie became the owner of a two-story house on Manor Square Drive just one block from her friend's new home. Harris County Appraisal District Records showed by 2002 that Julie's home was worth $155,560. Gail's townhouse was valued at $206,580.

Julie also wound up with the house in Harbor Park after the Knights' property was divvied up by the courts and Chuck had to move out. He and Laurie Wells moved into a smaller home together after coming out on the

short end of the settlements in their respective
divorces. Even with all that taken care of, the
brouhaha between the battling Knights and
the Bridges was far from over.

Shortly after Gail and Julie made a trip to the
District Attorney's offices, a grand jury in
Galveston indicted their husbands on felony
charges of unlawful interruption of oral or electronic communication. The women claimed
that Chuck and Steve taped their telephone
calls and spliced the conversations together to
make it seem they were making sexually sug-
gestive remarks and having adulterous affairs.
The charges against Steve were later dismissed
because of insufficient evidence. Early in 2003
the charges against Chuck were still pending.

Julie was back in court in January 2002,
this time with a lawsuit filed against her ex-
husband and several other parties whom she
blamed in one way or another for alleged links
to the reputed wire-tapping affair. Named with
Chuck were Laurie Wells, Steve Bridges, former League City neighbor Natasha Warren and
State Farm Lloyd's of Texas.

Julie alleged in the filing that the group placed
recording or microphone devices in her former
home in League City and at Gail Bridges' home
"for the express purposes of intercepting and/or

attempting to intercept communication between the plaintiffs and any other party with whom they were communicating."

Julie said she moved out of the house after learning of the recordings in May 1999. She also claimed that after Chuck left and she returned to her former home, she discovered that it had been ransacked and damaged. When she filed an insurance claim for damages, her husband slowed down an equitable settlement, she added.

Responding to the lawsuit alleging he and the others were involved in a wiretapping scheme, Steve declared that the action was "absolutely groundless."

Months after the divorces were finalized, the real-life soap opera took another crazy turn when Gail and Julie disguised themselves with wigs and dark glasses to appear together on television's *The Sally Jessy Raphael Show*. Gail used the pseudonym "Leslie," and Julie appeared as "Lisa." Their voices were also altered when the April 2001 TV show titled "My Husband Spies On Me" was broadcast. The young Texas moms talked about their husbands allegedly spying on them and didn't go into the more lurid accusations of lesbianism.

By the time the smoke began to settle a bit after nearly two years of domestic disputes, everyone involved was left badly battered and bruised. The breakups and the marital skirmishes they spawned were a nightmare that seemed to have no end. The emotional and economic consequences of the bitter divorces were tough on everybody and no one came out unscathed.

After the divorce, Gail still lived in League City, but she no longer fit quite so smoothly into the fast-paced glamorous world of young professionals and their families. She still had custody of two of her kids. She also managed to hang on to her Lincoln Navigator and $17,000 worth of personal jewelry, but money was tighter and she no longer had the luxury of being a full-time mom and homemaker.

Gone, too, was the imposing two-story, red brick house with the neatly manicured yards the family lived in together before her marriage was shattered. Her new house had no security gates around it, as had the home she had lived in with Steve and the kids at South Shore Harbor. And it was no longer as easy to plan leisurely tennis or shopping outings and casual lunches with her chum Julie.

At 38, Gail suddenly found herself as a single mother and she needed a job.

CHAPTER 4

Trouble in paradise

The new receptionist hired in August 2001 at Space Center Orthodontics appeared to be just the woman everyone in the busy office was looking for.

She was neatly dressed, efficient, energetic and eager to accept a salary that worked out to just $1,800 a month. Gail would never be able to match her previous lifestyle on the paycheck, but the job provided a handy re-entry into the workaday world where she could keep her eye out for new opportunities. She launched herself into the demanding routine of the busy orthodontics office with a burst of enthusiasm and high hopes for the future.

The next 11 months were also busy and challenging for David and Clara. While overseeing the management of eight dental clinics, including the two they practiced in, they began work on a major expansion project with the purchase of a large chunk of undeveloped property in a more exclusive area of shops and professional offices. They planned to construct a 6,000-square-foot dental clinic there and move each of their practices into the new building so they could work under the same roof.

David and Clara were earning excellent money, but their new investments were outpacing their immediate income and they borrowed from local banks to finance the rapidly expanding chain of dental clinics and the new building. David pledged $778,000 from a life insurance policy to Bank of America as collateral for one of the loans. Clara was the sole beneficiary of the policy.

When Lindsey advised her father that she wanted to become an orthodontist like he was, David and Clara assured the eager teenager that there would always be a space available there for her to join the family practice. Lindsey was still spending summers with her father and was obtaining practical experience helping out at Space Center Orthodontics during the long school break.

A pretty girl with long, lustrous hair and a slender, athletic build that fit perfectly with her role back in Columbus as a high school cheerleader, Lindsey was sweet 16 that summer. She had also inherited some of her father's love for music and was skilled on the violin and she got along so well with her stepmother that she called her "Mom."

But Clara was also mom to two healthy toddlers and even though they had a nanny, caring for the boys added to the family and business demands on her time and attention. Between treating dental patients, keeping track of the family business and spending quality time with the twins, she simply didn't have as much time to spend with David as she had earlier in their marriage.

Committed to doing her best with all the demands life presented, Clara was still careful to wind up her work at the office in time to drive the approximately 40 miles to their home at Polly Ranch Estates and personally cook the family supper every night — making sure to include David's favorites in the menu as often as possible. But there wasn't much time or opportunity anymore for after-dinner cuddling and long, intimate conversations about their lives together. Some nights Clara was so occupied with the boys that she fell asleep in their room and David wound up sleeping by himself.

Occupied as she was with her busy schedule, Clara allowed her weight to creep up a bit. At 44, she was still a handsome woman who dressed well — fashionably conservative — but she was no longer the sleek, young, long-legged beauty who captured the crown as Miss Colombia Houston and won David's heart.

Clara noticed that her husband seemed to be a bit more stressed out and wasn't as tolerant of the little -boy rowdiness of their sons. He didn't spend as much time playing with the boys or reading to them as he had only a few weeks earlier and he was showing a preference for keeping to himself.

David was also busy and had such a full plate with his orthodontics practice and the demands of the new office building under construction that his behavior change seemed to be perfectly understandable. Clara had upclose personal knowledge of exactly how stressful their hectic life was while attempting to juggle the demands of business and family.

David's usually placid personality continued to change and he became more irritable and difficult to please. He made it known that he was angered when an employee defaulted on an auto loan Clara co-signed. Clara still owed $65,000 on her own car, the 2000 silver Mercedes.

Then Clara took time off to attend a dental convention and after that she flew to Colombia for the wedding of a cousin, adding to her husband's growing irritation. The timing was especially bad because Clara had taken a month-long hiatus from her busy personal dental practice while they were hustling to scrape up as much cash as they could gather to finance the expensive new clinic construction project. Just when they needed money the most, she was spending money, not bringing any in.

David began grumbling to friends and employees that his wife wasn't as attentive and loving as she was before the boys were born and she didn't seem to appreciate him anymore.

No one showed much concern about the husbandly grousing until the new receptionist arrived and began openly flirting with the boss. David liked the attention and he was bowled over by the tantalizing sexiness of the pretty divorcee.

He began hanging around Gail's desk in the

front office, chatting and joking with her. For the first time, he began to reject the two- and three-times daily telephone calls from his wife. He instructed employees to tell Clara he was busy with a patient or otherwise occupied and couldn't take the calls. At other times, he simply left her on hold until she grew impatient and hung up.

In late February after Gail had worked at Space Center Orthodontics for about seven months, David asked her to have lunch with him at Perry's Grille and Steakhouse. She was perky, vivacious and skilled in sending out the subtle, and not so subtle, signals of romantic attraction and seduction. David was enchanted by the luring temptress and lunches at the popular Clear Lake area eatery quickly became a regular event.

David was boss of an office full of women and they were uncomfortable watching the flirtation between their boss and his attractive receptionist develop into a full-blown romantic affair. Gail stoked their concern by casually mentioning every once in a while that the boss was taking her to lunch.

At times when David treated his employees to lunch at a nearby restaurant, Gail hurried to beat the rest of the staff out the door so she could pop into the front seat of the Suburban and ride beside the boss. Her behavior wasn't missed by the other women as Gail familiarly patted him on the chest, then fiddled with coins in the truck's console. One of the women later huffed that she had worked for "Dr. David" for four years "and I didn't know where things were in his truck."

Gail was becoming increasingly open about the affair and she confided to some fellow employees that their boss told her he loved her. Then she revealed that he had shared a special confidence, telling her that he was no longer in love with his wife and was staying with her only because of their business partnership and the twins.

David had taken Gail to the Galleria, Houston's famous upscale shopping mall, in May when they went to bed together for the first time after checking into one of the two Westin hotels that are part of the complex of more than 300 retail stores and restaurants attractively festooned around a sparkling indoor ice-skating rink.

Within another two or three months, they were sneaking off for sex at some of the most expensively luxurious hotels in the Houston area, including the Nassau Bay Hilton, which had rooms overlooking the sprawling Johnson Space Center and the scenic waters of Clear Lake. The Hilton was also the high-rise hotel where David and Clara were married and hosted their wedding reception.

By most standards, David was already a wealthy man. The family's combined dental practice was raking in $650,000 a year and he and Clara had accumulated real estate, personal property and cash worth millions more.

There were no hot-pillow motels that charged by the hour, stocked pornographic videos for the VCRs in each room and had a parking lot full of rusting pickup trucks for Dr. David Harris and the stylish brunette who was his mistress. He could afford to travel first class. And they didn't revitalize themselves after bedroom acrobatics with double cheeseburgers and fries picked up at a drive-thru window. They shared drinks and dined together on choice cuisine in some of the finest and most popular local restaurants.

Diana Sherrill handled public relations for the rapidly growing dental clinic chain and in June she moved temporarily from Clara's office in Lake Jackson to Space Center Orthodontics at the southeast edge of Houston. She didn't like what she discovered going on between her boss and the bubbly new receptionist.

Other employees were also obviously uncomfortable and some of them became physically ill after witnessing the office hanky-panky. The seamy romantic intrigue was poisoning the atmosphere at the office and even patients were beginning to notice and talk.

The women who worked in the office knew their boss's wife and worried about her marriage. They realized that David would be quite a catch for any woman — especially a middle-age divorcée with three kids. But they needed their jobs and they knew better than to ask the boss to sit down for a little talk about his shabby behavior. It wasn't their place. Regardless of whether they liked or approved of Gail, most of them were civil to her because they felt they had to be.

After the intense pressure of two years of near nonstop squabbling and courtroom brawling with her husband, Gail also enjoyed the attention from a man who wasn't confrontational or downright hostile. David, in fact, treated her very well. A few weeks after she started to work for him, her salary was bumped up by $200 to $2,000 a month. She also began receiving monthly bonuses for her performance that sometimes amounted to as much as $500. No other front-office employees were receiving similar perks.

While sneaking around and living the high life with his mistress, David took another step out of his workaholic mold by taking up piano playing again for the first time since leaving high school. He resumed lessons with a piano teacher in Friendswood and showed promise of developing into a first-rate pianist. One time he even showed off his generosity and pleasure with his personal progress by offering the use of his new $89,000 tricentennial edition Steinway piano and home to his teacher for an adult recital. Steinway made only 300 of the limited edition instruments and only four were offered for sale in the Houston area. But when he walked into the Forshey Piano Company to look it over and try it out, the woman on his arm wasn't his wife, Clara. It was his receptionist, Gail.

The affair was becoming about as open as it could get without placing an advertisement in the newspaper. The lovers openly fondled each other and one employee repeatedly turned off a video camera that David's brother, Gerald Harris Jr., installed in the office to help figure out ways to improve interaction between patients and staff. Gerald was a psychologist who taught at the University of Houston and the employee didn't want him to see his little brother flirting so openly with the sexy sloe-eyed receptionist.

Lindsey was working in the office and at 16, she was old enough to figure out that something fishy was going on between her father and his vivacious employee. Her suspicions mounted when she saw him place his hand affectionately on Gail's leg.

Another time, according to later court testimony, while David was hanging around the front office Gail leaned over to retrieve files from a drawer and hoisted her bottom tantalizingly into the air in front of her boss's face. David seemed to appreciate the exhibition and stared with open admiration.

Lindsey was upset by the blatant display and by her father's appreciative reaction. A dental clinic executive named Susan Hanson was also concerned and attempted to talk to the teenager to console her. It appeared to Susan that Clara had been pushed into the backseat of the relationship. Dr. David's wife clearly wasn't No. 1 in his affections anymore.

Over the Fourth of July holiday in 2002 while employees at Space Center Orthodontics and the Jackson Dental Clinic were uneasily fretting about their employers' marriage, the Harris family took a break from the hectic work schedule and flew off for a tropical vacation of sun, water and sand in Jamaica. David, Clara, Lindsey and the twins relaxed together during the brief Caribbean island getaway. But when they returned to Texas and resumed work after the mini-vacation, it was back to the same old routine for David and Gail.

Some longtime employees of David's had been hoping he would return from the vacation as a changed man who was once again devoted to his wife and family. They soon reluctantly decided there was nothing to do but confront their boss about Gail.

The two-timing orthodontist admitted being involved, but balked at a suggestion that he fire his girlfriend. He insisted that he was still committed to his marriage and loved his wife, but wasn't ready to dump Gail from her job and from his life.

Diana Sherrill, the PR rep, was so upset by the seamy affair that she returned to Lake Jackson Dental Care on July 16. Once back in the less tense, more placid surroundings, she tried to diplomatically warn Clara that there were problems with her marriage that needed to be addressed.

"I told her she needed to protect her marriage, not to ignore anything out of the ordinary," Sherrill later testified in court. "Pay attention to Dr. David, maybe get to counseling. I wanted her to be able to start seeing the things I had seen."

By this time, other employees had also dropped cautious hints that something was wrong, but Clara refused to admit she had a problem. She trusted her husband and assured her concerned friends that he would never stray. The frank discussion with Sherrill, however, which occurred while the two women shared dinner, left little room for continued denial. After their meal, the friends went to a nearby salon where Clara had her hair cut and colored. While the hair stylist worked on Clara's hair, she was apparently thinking over the discussion and her relationship with her husband.

Returning home about 10 p.m., she and David had a talk about her returning to the house so late. The talk wasn't heated, but they had a few things to iron out and Clara asked her husband point-blank if he still loved her. He hesitated, then looked at her with what she perceived to be a question mark on his face. For the first time, she felt in her heart that her husband wasn't sure if he loved her or not.

One of Clara's chums from the orthodontics office had already confronted David with an ultimatum to tell his wife what was going on or else the friend would do the job for him. But the late Tuesday evening talk with his wife when he left her question about their relationship

unanswered must also have had a lot to do with
his decision the next morning to clear the air.

Clara was preparing for work and about to
step into the shower when David walked into
the bathroom with a troubled look on his face.
She asked him what the trouble was and he
said he needed to tell her something but didn't
know how to say it.

"Is it that hard to tell?" she asked as they sat
next to each other on the edge of the bathtub.

"I think you have to know. There is somebody
else," he confessed.

When she asked who her rival was, he told her
he was having an affair with his receptionist, but
claimed they hadn't been to bed with each other.
He had lunches with Gail, but their most intimate
encounter occurred when he kissed her on the
hand. David said he wasn't sure if he loved her.

Although David was lying and would soon be
admitting to far more intimate activities with
the pretty receptionist, he had already said
more than enough to convince his wife that
their marriage was in serious trouble.

Clara was stunned by the surprise revelation.
She asked again if he still loved her.

"I don't know," he confessed.

Clara began sobbing and shaking. She had
always believed that their marriage was special

and they would grow old together. Choking back her tears, she warned that she would have to get a divorce. David replied that he would "do anything" to avoid breaking up the marriage.

Dressing quickly, the shaken wife walked downstairs, found Lindsey in the kitchen and told her that her father was having an affair with his receptionist.

The teenager replied that she already knew, adding that everybody in her father's office knew.

Reeling from the emotional double-whammy, Clara marched back upstairs and slapped her husband. David had practiced unarmed martial arts and as she reached for his hair he grabbed her arm and slammed her onto her back. Clara found herself lying on the floor holding his toupee in her hand.

David was as shocked as she was by the violence and both of them quieted down and began to talk things over like rational adults. They decided to try and work things out.

Lindsey also tried to help. She loved her father but disapproved of the affair and the way he was treating his wife.

"Don't do this to her. This is wrong," she pleaded with him. "You guys love each other!"

David told his daughter that he knew that, but she didn't understand because she didn't

live with them all the time. He complained that
he didn't get any attention from his wife.

Clara telephoned Lake Jackson Dental Care
and canceled her appointments for the next two
weeks. Then she climbed into the Mercedes
with her husband and her stepdaughter and
drove to Space Center Orthodontics to fire Gail.

David looked crestfallen while the unhappy
trio headed for the showdown. Lindsey later
recalled that her father didn't want Gail to go,
but her mother was adamant that the receptionist had to be fired. "To save our marriage,
we need to get rid of her now," Clara insisted.

From a solely business viewpoint, even if
David had refused to let Gail go from Space
Center Orthodontics, as the controlling partner of the corporation with 51 percent of the
stock, Clara had the authority to fire her.

After pulling into a parking place at Space
Center Orthodontics and storming into the
office, Clara summoned her rival to an empty
room for a talk. When the two women disappeared inside, Clara slammed the door so hard
that a clock fell off the wall.

Dejected and embarrassed, David waited
outside the room with his daughter and other
members of the staff. The eyeball-to-eyeball
confrontation didn't last very long and within a

few minutes Gail emerged from the room and began cleaning out her desk.

Soon enough — once things quieted down — David would be contacting his mistress again.

CHAPTER 5

Whatever
it takes

Clara blamed herself for neglecting her appearance and her husband, but she wasn't about to roll over and play dead while he tap-danced off with a rival — Gail Bridges — or any other woman who saw him as an opportunity that was too good to pass up.

David had confessed his admiration for his girlfriend's prominent breasts and slender, petite body and after the drive home, Clara took the first desperate steps in a self-improvement program aimed at saving her marriage.

She telephoned a plastic surgeon with offices next door to Space Center Orthodontics and scheduled a breast enlargement operation. She also determined to lose weight, work out and get herself in better shape. And she promised David that she would give up her own dental practice so she could be waiting for him in their home when he returned from work. Lindsey tried to help out by giving her stepmother a couple of books about repairing damaged relationships.

The distressed wife was confident that her unwavering love could bring them through the crisis in their marriage. They had worked and prayed together while striving to become parents and accomplished their goal. She was convinced they could also repair the emotional damage from her inattention and David's straying to triumph again.

On the evening of July 18, the day after the confrontation with Gail at David's office, Clara and her husband left Lindsey and the boys to drive to a nice piano bar somewhere and talk things over. They couldn't find one and after looking for a while they settled for a sports bar near the Houston airport, pulled the Mercedes into a parking space and walked inside the darkened saloon.

While other patrons stared vacantly at television sets tuned to the Astros, sipped at frosty Red Star beers or cool Coronas and debated batting and earned run averages, the troubled couple sat in a booth a few feet away trying to figure out what was wrong with their marriage and what they could do to fix it.

David was brutally frank. He complained that Clara was overweight, talked too much, was addicted to her job and was too controlling and bossy. He carped that she didn't let him do what he wanted to do. By comparison, he said, Gail was easygoing and let him call the shots. Clara always took it on herself to plan vacations and other family events or activities, he complained. David said he also disliked his wife's habit of interrupting him when he was speaking. Gail never did that.

He griped that Clara was too extravagant while decorating and furnishing their house, spent way too much on toys for the boys and needed to show more spending restraint — like Gail. The pretty receptionist was frugal and tight with her money.

David didn't mention his expensive new

$89,000 Steinway or that it was Clara who urged him to indulge himself and buy it.

As he contrasted the attributes and negatives of his wife and his younger mistress, Clara dutifully jotted down the match-ups on a couple of bar napkins. She listed the following point-by-point comparisons in two lines as:

General Clara	General Gail
Loud	Good conversationalist
Smiles more now	Smiles a lot
Will have big boobs in a few days	Big boobs
Fat	Not fat, perfect body
Pretty feet and hands	Feet and hands not pretty
Pretty eyes	Nice hair
Large person, too big	Perfect nose
Good values, not a fanatic	Good values
Spends a lot of money	Manages a tight budget
	Petite, perfect to sleep with all night

"I would love ... you when you get your boobs to just be around the house waiting for me," he told his concerned spouse.

It was a demeaning experience that would hurt the pride of any woman whose husband was sitting with her over drinks comparing her with his mistress — and not comparing her well. But Clara swallowed her humiliation, choked back the tears and vowed to herself to live up to her husband's expectations. He was the love of her life and she was ready to do whatever it took to keep him and preserve their marriage.

During the next few days she greeted David at home when he returned from work, cooked his favorite meals and had sex with him three times a night. She also bought a $1,277.25 one-year fitness club membership and hired a personal trainer to help firm up her figure, lightened her hair to reddish blonde, began going to a tanning salon, abandoned her stylishly conservative wardrobe for tighter, more provocative outfits, splurged on hundreds of dollars worth of sexy lingerie at a Victoria's Secret shop and wrote out a $5,000 check as a down payment for the breast implants — and a tummy tuck. Then she walked to the salon on the other side of her husband's office and got a set of new nails.

As Clara struggled to repair the agonizing rift in her marriage, she organized a weekend trip for the family to nearby Galveston. After a comfortable drive down Interstate 45, the Harris' snacked on seafood, walked along the beaches overlooking the sparkling waters of the Gulf of Mexico and snapped family photographs.

Clara was apparently taking other steps, as well, to deal with the threat to her marriage and family security. There were reportedly complaints to police that Clara was telephoning and making terrorist-style threats on Gail's life. But a friend of Clara's claimed the calls weren't threatening at all; she had merely called to thank her husband's mistress for opening her eyes.

The heartsick homemaker did her best to show a brave face and turn her marriage around, but the shock of David's philandering and her frenzied efforts to remake herself into the woman he claimed to have wanted her to be took a devastating emotional and physical toll.

"She couldn't eat — I don't think it was a diet," Susan Hanson later recalled. "She was consumed by what was going on." Clara lost a dress size in a single week, her friend estimated.

The troubled couple even sat down with David's parents and with Lindsey to confess to the sordid affair. It was wretched news and David asked for forgiveness. But he also pleaded that as an important part of the healing process, he needed to take Gail to a restaurant for one last late luncheon together so he could apologize for all the anger, embarrassment and other distressing fallout from their relationship because the trouble wasn't her fault.

Reluctantly, Clara agreed to a meeting between her husband and "the other woman" to clear the air once and for all. According to *Texas Monthly*, which quoted a "close friend," Clara even told her husband that if he kept his word and helped preserve the marriage he could continue some kind of friendship with his former mistress.

The meeting was to be at the couple's old trysting place, Perry's Grille and Steakhouse, early Wednesday evening, July 24.

CHAPTER 6

Blue Moon

Clara was troubled by second thoughts over her consent to a final meeting between her husband and the stylish brunette who had stolen his heart.

Honestly, she was never comfortable with the decision to begin with. After all, David had betrayed her once already and he was explicitly tactless while describing the other woman's sensual charms during the humiliating discussion at the sports bar. Clara decided she needed professional help to deal with the crisis in her marriage and she wasn't thinking about a shrink.

Flipping through the Yellow Pages, she found an advertisement for "Blue Moon Investigations," a private detective agency headquartered in Webster. A blurb on the firm's Internet Web page early in 2003 described Blue Moon as offering "professional and discreet investigation services. Utilizing the latest in investigative methods, equipment and database searches, Blue Moon is on the cutting edge of the private investigation industry." Blue Moon was "one of the largest, most respectable investigative firms in the industry in Texas, Nationwide and Worldwide," it was added.

The private detective agency offered a wide variety of services, including different types of investigations. Missing persons investigations, accident investigations — and domestic surveillance — were all important components listed on the company menu. Domestic investigations accounted for a huge chunk of the firm's business; flaps much like the Harris case appeared to be. Blue Moon clients have included business executives, educators and the wife of at least one astronaut.

Inserting themselves into domestic squabbles to get the goods on a wife or husband suspected of cheating can be a cash cow for private eyes. Investigators are known for pulling out all the stops short of crossing the line into illegality to get the job done. Word gets around quickly and a reputation for successfully collecting evidence against a cheating spouse, especially when it includes incriminating still photographs, video and audio tapes, can produce a steady stream of new clients for years to come. Sometimes the same client will show up a few months or years after first hiring an agency and sign a contract with the same sleuths to shadow a new spouse.

If one partner to a divorce can show that the other was sleeping around or guilty of such offensive behavior as cruelty, mental cruelty, abandonment or drug addiction, the information can provide the injured party with a big leg up on a better than normal 50-50 split of cash and property. If children are involved, it can tip the scales favorably in custody matters.

When Clara first walked into Bobbi Bacha's Blue Moon Investigations office, she didn't behave as if she was motivated by concern over getting her share, or more, of cash and property after a split with her husband. She was already the majority owner of their corporation and had proven that she was perfectly capable of supporting herself and the boys with her personal dental practice.

She wanted to prove beyond a shadow of a doubt that David was being dishonest with her and still slipping around with his sexy girlfriend because she wanted to preserve her marriage, not dissolve it.

According to accounts, Clara walked into the agency's second floor offices on Tuesday, July 23, and told a woman at the front desk that she wanted her husband tailed on Wednesday night.

Clara explained that David planned to meet his mistress at Perry's Grille and Steakhouse and she wanted a report on their conversation. Clara was a bit teary-eyed when she sat down with PI Claudine Phillips, but that wasn't unusual for Blue Moon clients with marital problems.

The troubled homemaker composed herself, however, as she got down to the nitty-gritty of the business at hand. As she retraced her husband's dalliance, she explained to the investigations coordinator that he was a good man who was naively allowing himself to be deceived by a calculating woman with an eye on his pocketbook.

Clara wanted a detective to keep an eye on him during the meeting at the restaurant Wednesday evening and then continue the surveillance on

Gail for the next couple of days. Perhaps because of her own role as a mother of young children, Clara added one caveat: she didn't want Gail tailed while she had her kids with her.

In a short time, Clara was passing on hearsay she had picked up about her rival, especially the gossip that Gail was a lesbian. She suspected Gail and the woman she was believed to be living with hatched a scheme to snag David and get his money, Clara said. He was being deceived and couldn't recognize what was going on because he was dazzled by a scheming woman who was using her predatory allure to make him think he was in love.

David's lover was an "evil" woman, Clara volunteered. And she wanted documentation to prove Gail was involved in a lesbian affair, so she could pass on the information to her husband and help him recognize the kind of woman he was infatuated with.

It wasn't the first time Blue Moon had been asked to dig up evidence that Gail and Julie were involved in a lesbian love affair. But investigators didn't recognize Gail's name as either the subject of one of their earlier investigations or as the woman who previously visited the offices with Julie Knight when the firm was hired to track Chuck. A misspelling of his last name on documents as "Night" instead of "Knight" may have been a factor.

Blue Moon's fee schedule for a domestic surveillance assignment called for a four-hour minimum at $55 an hour. Clara wanted her husband and his girlfriend tailed for much longer than four hours and wrote out a check for $1,547.98 to cover the various charges.

An important provision of the contract required the client to agree not to show up at the scene of a stakeout. The contract made it plain that if Clara violated the provision, all bets were off. Blue Moon would drop the investigation and she would lose any refunds.

There was good reason for the rule against showing up at the scene of a stakeout, because a nasty divorce, especially when adultery is involved, can make an emotional wreck out of a wronged spouse and leave nerves and emotions raw and dangerously on edge. If the husband or wife is on the scene to catch their partner in flagrant cheating, there is a good chance of violence.

Clara attempted to hold her head high as she walked out of the investigative agency offices after receiving assurance that her husband and his girlfriend would be placed under close surveillance the following night.

There was still one small detail to take care

of. Clara was so emotionally scrambled when she fired Gail from Space Center Orthodontics that she couldn't even remember what the woman looked like. Clara telephoned Blue Moon about 4:30 the next afternoon and said she wanted to drop off a photograph of her rival and give investigators the license plate number of her husband's car. She showed up at the office with her stepdaughter and Phillips, a 32-year veteran of the detective business, later recalled that Lindsey was "very teenagerish" at the meeting and appeared to think "it was cool" being in the office of a real-life professional gumshoe. The gravity of the situation didn't seem to have sunk in for the girl, Phillips said.

During her second meeting with the investigators, Clara temporarily lost her composure and sobbingly blurted out, "You're my best friends." Before she could be handed a box of tissues kept handy for clients, she recovered her composure.

Gail's name still didn't strike a bell with Bobbi and the Blue Moon staff and they still didn't know what she looked like because Clara didn't, after saying she would, provide them with a picture.

Bobbi assured Clara she could proceed anyway. Having established Blue Moon in 1995, the

43-year-old professional snoop had seen pictures of a lot of mistresses and philandering husbands in her time. She was herself a two-time loser in the marriage stakes and worked as a secretary for a detective agency before stepping up to become a private investigator, then getting it right the third time by tying the knot with Lucas Bacha. Lucas was a Boeing engineer, but after his wife opened Blue Moon he was good about filling in when he was needed to help around the office or do surveillance work.

When working on domestic investigations, Bobbi believed that females were more observant and especially more likely to notice small details. So although her husband sometimes helped out and her chief investigator was once a male stripper, Blue Moon was heavily staffed with women; including schoolteachers, secretaries and college students. When Clara went to Blue Moon for help, the agency could call on 38 assistant investigators.

Bobbi was a good role model for her employees when it came to dogged determination to get the goods on a suspected wrongdoer. On one case, where the wife and girlfriend ganged up on a wealthy Houston car dealer after learning he was deceiving both of them, the queen-size sleuth scooted under a table with a tape recorder while the wronged spouse hid in a closet. Then the girlfriend maneuvered the husband onto the bed in her apartment while Bobbi taped the pillow talk and the outraged wife eavesdropped.

David's Wednesday night surveillance was assigned to Lindsey Ann Dubec, an enthusiastic and energetic 22-year-old University of Houston-Clear Lake criminal justice major with a long ponytail. She neither looked nor behaved like the classic private eye of modern literature and film, who is typically depicted as a grizzled, hard-drinking male with an ever-present cigarette stub dangling from the edge of his mouth and something going on with his leggy secretary.

Dubec drove to Space Center Orthodontics, where she picked up David's trail when he left his office. He didn't drive to Perry's Grille as expected. Instead, he made a beeline for the Nassau Bay Hilton and met Gail at the hotel restaurant.

The young PI couldn't get close enough to overhear their conversation while they chatted and sipped drinks, but it wasn't long before Gail stood up and walked out. David followed and caught up with her when she reached her car in the employee parking lot at the rear of the building.

Friends were later quoted as saying that David pleaded to keep the affair going and promised that he could continue to arrange discreet meetings. Gail reportedly replied that she wouldn't settle for sneaking around while he was still married.

Whatever his response to that was, it must have been convincing, because after a few more minutes of conversation they turned and walked back inside the hotel together. David approached the front desk and requested "a nice room." He signed for it with a false name and paid cash.

After the couple disappeared behind the elevator doors, Dubec walked back outside and moved her car to a position where she had a good view of the front entrance to the Hilton and of David's Suburban in the parking lot. Then she prepared a video camera she brought along to record the couple as they emerged from the hotel. Bobbi taught her investigators to capture film of the subjects they had under surveillance whenever possible.

While the young PI settled down in her gray Toyota Camry for what looked like a long wait, she telephoned a girlfriend. The chum drove to the Hilton with sandwiches and soft drinks to ride shotgun and chat with her friend during the stakeout.

Back at the Polly Ranch Estates, Clara's belief that her husband was at a restaurant having a cozy tete-a-tete with the woman who was at the center of so much of the Harris family misery was too much to bear. She couldn't simply sit home and stare at inane television sitcoms while desperately trying to blot visual images from her mind of David and his pleasingly chatty mistress — who was just the right size to hold and cuddle all night. Although Clara was made up with a heavy application of mascara and other cosmetics that were part of her campaign to win back her cheating husband, she was dressed casually in a turquoise T-shirt and blue jeans when she invited Lindsey to ride along while she drove to Perry's Grille to look for David.

After the birth of the boys, Clara hadn't been as attentive to Lindsey as she was during early summer and Christmas visits, but the trouble had restored some of their former closeness. The teenager was now being cast in a role as her stepmother's trusted confidante.

David and Gail weren't at Perry's Grille, so the two drove to three other restaurants where the straying husband had said he and Gail sometimes billed and cooed. They weren't there either, so Clara drove to Gail's house. Neither Gail's black Lincoln Navigator nor David's Chevrolet Impala were parked in the driveway. Gail had traded in her red Navigator for a new one, colored a less conspicuous black after her divorce.

It was about 8 p.m. when Clara telephoned Blue Moon to find out what was going on and demanded to know where her wandering spouse was. Lucas Bacha was fielding evening emergency calls and although he didn't know where David was, he agreed to call the investigator trailing him and get back to Clara. Bacha called Dubec, who said she was outside a hotel waiting for David and Gail to come out.

Bacha got back in touch with Clara and told her that her husband was at a hotel. He apparently didn't name the hotel, but he didn't have to. After listening to her husband's embarrassingly detailed confessions of his affair, Clara had a good idea where to look.

She telephoned her nanny, Maria Gonzalez, and instructed her to pack an old suitcase with enough of David's suits and other clothing to last him a week, then to leave it on the doorstep. The rest of his clothes and personal effects were to be dumped in the trash.

Then Clara steered her Mercedes through the moist early evening gloom toward the Nassau Bay Hilton at 3000 NASA Road 1.

CHAPTER 7

"It's over"

The woman and the girl had barely turned off NASA Road 1 and into the hotel grounds before Lindsey spotted the black Navigator in the parking lot. The emotional hysteria lurking just below the surface while Clara struggled to maintain an aura of calm and decorum was about to burst.

Clara stopped her Mercedes, slid out of her

seat and walked to the SUV with her car keys in
her hand. She raked the keys along the driver's
side of Gail's car, smashed out the taillights,
broke a tailgate hitch, kicked in the grill, ripped
the windshield wiper from the rear window
and furiously twisted the front wipers.

Then she stalked back to the Mercedes, drove
to the guest parking area at the front of the hotel
and pulled into an empty parking space.
Moments later the angry wife and the teenager
entered the hotel lobby and walked to the front
desk. About one hour earlier David and Gail had
ridden an elevator upstairs to a sixth-floor room.

Paul Garrett Clark was on duty as front desk
clerk and recalled in later courtroom testimony
that the teenager told him her brother was sick
and she needed to locate her father. She asked
him to check the registry for a David Harris. A
couple of clicks on the computer revealed that
no one was registered by that name. So the girl
asked him to check the names David Bridges,
Gail Bridges and Gail Harris. None of the
names produced a match.

Clark remembered seeing the two women,
whom he assumed to be mother and daughter,
at the hotel the previous day. They ate at the
hotel restaurant and it appeared the older
woman was crying and being comforted by the

teenager. Before leaving the hotel the older woman had approached the front desk, inquired about the room rates and asked to see a suite. He was unaware that she only wanted a look so that she would have a better idea of the layout of the love-nest favored by her adulterous husband and his girlfriend. Now the women were back.

Clara knew her husband was there. She came up with a plan to smoke him out by telephoning him on his cell phone and telling him that one of the twins was sick and he needed to come home. Both wife and daughter relayed the same distressing message in separate calls.

David said he was at Pappadeaux, another area restaurant that Clara and Lindsey had missed checking out. He promised he would be right home.

Clara's frustration and fury was building a few minutes later when the elevator doors opened and the lovers stepped out into the lobby holding hands. Clara later recalled that her love rival had "a Mona Lisa smile" on her face.

"You bitch, he's my husband," Clara screamed as she launched herself at the surprised woman. Clark looked up from his front desk computer station as Clara landed a solid punch in Gail's face. When the smaller woman reeled back and tumbled to the floor, Clara punched

her in the face again, grabbed a handful of hair
and began ripping at her blouse while continuing to yell. David's lover was taken totally by
surprise and desperately struggled to protect
herself from the raging spitfire who was
pounding her face and body. Gail clutched the
other end of her blouse and held on for dear
life, trying to shield herself from more blows
while preserving her modesty and preventing
her clothes from being torn from her body.

"This is Dr. David Harris and he's f***ing this
woman right here," Clara screeched.

While the older women tangled in a flurry of
flailing arms and legs, torn clothing, scraggly
hair and screeches, Lindsey rushed at her
father, striking at him with her purse. "I hate
you! I hate you! I hate you!" she screamed.

Lindsey had broken down into tears and
David was standing off to the side watching the
brawl when Clark leaped over the front desk
and scrambled across the lobby floor to the
fiercely struggling women. It seemed that the
job of separating them was up to him, because
no one else was doing a thing to stop the brawl.

"It looked pretty serious," the young hotel
employee later recalled.

The desk clerk couldn't pry the combatants
apart, so he did the only thing he thought he

could do to protect the smaller woman from the furious rain of blows. He squeezed between them and sprawled on top of Gail to protect her with his own body. Seconds later he was jolted with three sharp punches to the right temple. Clara was still throwing roundhouses as another hotel employee telephoned Nassau Bay police and asked for help.

Meanwhile, other startled employees and guests who had been working or strolling in the lobby of the upscale hotel watched the uneven contest in amazement and alarm.

John Tyler, a 31-year-old public affairs specialist with the Baylor College of Medicine, had already climbed into his car with some friends after attending a Bible study class when he heard a woman screaming and ran toward the entrance. Just inside the lobby door a woman was battering another woman with her fists and screaming, "You bitch! He's my husband!"

A man had his hands around the waist of the screaming attacker and was attempting to drag her off the woman who was on the receiving end of the battering. David had finally stepped into the fight.

Tyler estimated that about 10 hotel employees tried to break up the fight, but every time the women were pulled apart the bigger woman started all over again. Tyler and a pal jumped in to help break things up. She was "very angry, very angry," he said of the aggressor.

David finally put an end to the fracas. He grabbed at Clara's face, shoved her violently onto the floor and kicked her.

Clark took the opportunity to help the petite and badly shaken loser to her feet and she asked him to "please help me get to my car. I've got to get out of here." Gail hadn't got off a single punch.

Other onlookers gathered up the contents of her purse that were scattered over the floor when it was ripped away during the struggle. After the cosmetics and other personal items were stuffed back into the bag, someone handed it to her.

Another guest at the hotel who witnessed the blowup was quoted in the press as saying that as David was leaving the hotel he snarled at his wife, "Goodbye, I'm leaving you."

"She seemed stunned and proceeded to scurry off to the car with her (step)daughter," the woman later recalled.

Evangelos Smiros, the hotel's food and beverage director, escorted Clara and Lindsey through the lobby to their car. Just outside the entrance, Clara hesitated and glared across the driveway at her husband.

David was following a few feet behind his

bedraggled, trembling girlfriend and her escort while she clutched at her ripped clothing and made her way unsteadily across the parking lot toward her parked SUV. He was steaming mad, his face purple with anger and he was yelling, "It's over! It's over! It's over!"

As David, Gail, hotel employees and guests spilled out of the front lobby entrance, Dubec and her friend saw the commotion and the young gumshoe reached for her video camera. Although it was about 9 p.m., the lobby entrance and the parking lot were well lit and she began rolling the film.

The unexpected events that occurred during the next few minutes seemed almost surreal and only bits and pieces were recorded by the camera as Clara's Mercedes roared out of the darkness, smashed into David and hurled his body through the air.

Shocked at the sudden violence, the two young women screamed, "Oh, my God! Oh, my God!" The video camera continued to roll.

At the rear of the hotel, out of sight of the PI and her camera, Clara had scooted behind the wheel of her silver sedan. On the outside, she appeared curiously calm, but her emotions were dangerously frayed and in turmoil. Lindsey was also shaken by the violence and emotional cataclysm when she opened the door on the front passenger side and slid in beside her stepmother.

The car backed normally out of the parking space. Then, while Smiros watched in sudden alarm, it "burned rubber" and with a screech of tires, lurched rapidly forward.

Smiros dashed after the speeding vehicle and banged on the trunk with his hand and yelled, "Stop! Stop!" while the silver Mercedes roared around a wall separating the parking areas and across the lot toward Gail's parked SUV.

Tyler and his friend were still standing near the entrance and thought the violence had ended at last when they heard the squeal of tires and saw a couple of hotel employees running after a speeding car roaring out of the darkness with its headlights on.

"She was actually driving into a crowd of people who were out there," the Bible student later said.

Tyler and other bystanders watched in shock and horror and Smiros heard a sickening "thump" as the heavy car slammed into David before the terrified man could scramble out of the way. "Oh, my God, she's hit him," hotel employees yelled.

Clark was standing near Gail's car when he heard a vehicle revving up and plunging toward them. The speeding vehicle brushed past him,

scraped the Navigator and smashed into the startled dentist, carrying him briefly on the hood,
then tossing him 25 feet or more through the air
and onto the pavement. "I looked up at David. He
had bulging eyes, a terrified look," Clark recalled.

Then as the hotel employees watched helplessly,
the heavy car careened around a grassy median
strip and ran over the body again and again.
Unable to get out of the speeding vehicle, the
teenager in the front passenger seat screamed in
horror, pleading with the driver to stop. "Please
stop! Please stop the car!" she cried. The furious
woman at the steering wheel was killing
Lindsey's dad and the horrified girl could feel the
bump every time the car jolted over his body but
couldn't do a thing about it except watch helplessly through the windshield — and scream.

What had begun as a typical golden summer
for the Midwest teenager in East Texas with
her father and his wife had turned into a living
nightmare. Clara was clutching the wheel
and staring straight ahead like a zombie while
turning the 4,000-pound luxury vehicle into a
lethal killing machine.

As the tennis players dashed from the lighted
courts across the street, Creger, Williams and
others also sprinted to the site of the impact.
It was already too late for the philandering

dentist. David's body and his mistress's car were a mess of mangled metal and bloody flesh.

Blake Duran, another hotel employee, watched helplessly as the driver of the Mercedes sprawled on top of the dying man's body and tearfully apologized, telling him how much she loved him.

Police switchboards in Nassau Bay and other nearby communities were lighting up with 911 calls and one man excitedly blurted out to the operator: "We have a guy in a car who went nuts. He ran over somebody."

Nassau Bay Police Department Patrolman Frank Reyna was the first law enforcement officer to arrive at the scene. The dying man was still crumpled amid the blood and gore in the parking lot.

A few feet away Clara cried uncontrollably while a hotel employee restrained her from returning to the crushed body of her husband. She sobbed that it was an accident when she rammed him with her car.

An ambulance rushed David to nearby St. John's hospital before police detectives or evidence technicians could photograph his crushed body at the scene. He was pronounced dead shortly after arrival at the hospital emergency room. He suffered multiple crushing injuries.

The distraught woman continued to sob but

didn't resist as Reyna handcuffed her and helped her into the backseat of his squad car for the drive to police headquarters so she could be questioned about the dreadful events. Once she was inside the car, Clara took several deep breaths to compose herself, then sat quietly. On the drive to police headquarters, Reyna didn't hear any more crying or observe any new tears.

According to Nassau Bay Police Lieutenant Joe M. Cashiola, the woman "looked like she was in shock. She didn't make any statements at the scene."

Gail was also driven to the police headquarters where homicide detectives tried to question her, but she was so shaken and woozy after the deadly rampage that they gave up. She was fading in and out of consciousness and complaining about being cold, so they sent her to a Clear Lake hospital. Doctors determined that she had a concussion and other injuries. Gail later testified in court that although she was only a few feet away from her lover when he was mowed down, she was "in a fog" and could offer no information about his death.

Late that night when Lindsey was driven home, she gathered up her father's clothes from a garbage can where the nanny had dumped them. The grieving teenager took them upstairs and laid them out on her bed. Then she rounded up other personal possessions of her father from his closet and bathroom and took them to her room.

Being so close to his things made her feel like he was there with her.

CHAPTER 8

Texas justice

Clara needed someone to talk to and homicide investigators were anxious to oblige when they sat down in an interrogation room about 5 a.m. Thursday morning to discuss the terrible tragedy that occurred the previous night.

As she told her story, the soiled and rumpled woman looked nothing like the beauty queen she once was. She hadn't come through the nasty dustup in the hotel lobby unscathed and bruises covered her face, arms, elbows and thighs.

Her face was the color of bread dough and a wasteland of creases, faded makeup and worry lines spread around eyes that clearly showed her shock and fatigue. The mascara she so painstakingly applied just a few hours earlier was smeared and spoiled. And the hair she lightened to blonde as part of her doomed "win back David" campaign drooped from her head in weary snarls.

Before there could be any serious talk, police had to read Clara the obligatory Miranda Warning, the notorious 1966 U.S. Supreme Court-crafted criminal escape hatch that everyone who has ever watched a cop show on television or the big screen is so familiar with.

The exact wording can differ slightly in various jurisdictions, but a typical message reads:

"You have the right to remain silent. Anything you say can and will be used against you in a court of law. You have the right to the presence of an attorney to assist you prior to questioning, and to be with you during questioning if you so desire. If you cannot afford an attorney, you have the right to have an attorney appointed for you prior to the questioning.

Do you understand these rights?"

Once Miranda was dealt with, homicide investigators recorded Clara's dreary recital while she began explaining that she was distraught over marital problems and hired a private detective agency to shadow her husband. She said that after catching him and Gail together at the hotel she wanted to separate them when she saw him helping his lover into the Lincoln.

But she never told police she wanted to kill him.

"She did admit doing it but she didn't say why," recalled Lieutenant Cashiola.

The ashen-faced woman in the wrinkled and soiled T-shirt and jeans was fingerprinted and stared forlornly into the camera while a police photographer snapped mug shots. Then she was directed to slip her simple gold wedding band from her finger and it was stored away with her cash and other valuables before she was locked in a cell in the women's section of the Harris County Jail in Houston.

After homicide investigators conferred with prosecutors, she was named on preliminary charges of murder.

Clara's treasured silver Mercedes was hauled away and impounded for inspection by forensics experts over the next several days. Detective Julio Cesar Rincones of the Webster Police Department and other forensics experts eventually

recovered a large patch of dried blood and bits of
hair and grass on the undercarriage. He bagged
the material as evidence. David's fingerprints
and two palm prints, one near the hood ornament and the other near the driver's side fender,
were found on the outside of the car.

Some of the most grisly evidence was recovered from the victim. Tire tracks were imbedded
on his body and the telltale marks were carefully
photographed by a professional police photographer. Other color photographs were also taken
of the crime scene, including the pooled blood on
the pavement, Gail's mangled black Navigator
and Clara's Mercedes. Close-ups were snapped
of the dents.

Nassau Bay Police Detective Theresa Relkin
collected, bagged and marked evidence at the
scene, including the tooth that Julie Creger set
aside on the cement after it dropped out of
David's mouth into her hand. A chunk of hair
ripped from his toupee and the two towels used
to wipe up his blood were also bagged.

When the death car was hauled away from the
hotel, an album of wedding photos and Clara's
checkbook for a joint Bank of America account
with her husband were left inside with other
personal belongings. She had jotted Gail's
name, telephone numbers and address on the

back inside cover. Check stubs made out to Victoria's Secret, the fitness center, a nail salon, spa, beauty parlor and various apparel shops provided sad evidence of the manic week-long self-improvement flurry she launched in the doomed effort to save her marriage.

Two stubs totaling $5,310 were made out to the same plastic surgeon and dated July 24, the day David died. Other stubs for checks written in the last few days were to Blue Moon Investigations and to the Harris' church for a building fund.

Gail's damaged SUV was also impounded and meticulously inspected by detectives and evidence technicians. The broken windshield wipers ripped off by Clara before going inside the hotel were collected as evidence and photographs were taken of the deep scratch marks along the sides and back made by Clara's car keys and of the later damage that occurred when the vehicle was sideswiped by the speeding Mercedes.

On Friday, the accused murderess appeared for a probable cause hearing before Texas State District Judge Carol G. Davies. Despite her weariness and the wrenching emotional pounding of the previous 48 hours, Clara looked more like her old self. She had spent the previous night at home, after being released from the

Harris County Jail on $30,000 bond. District
Court judges used a fee schedule that stipulated
$30,000 for defendants charged with murder.

The defendant's hair was neatly swept back at
the nape of her neck, she was dressed in a stylish black pantsuit and she stood stoically erect
while responding to questions from the bench
in a voice that was subdued but unwavering.

David's 72-year-old father attended the hearing with other family members and looked on
quietly as the prosecution briefly detailed the
alleged offense and explained to the court why
they believed the defendant should be held
over for trial. A court order was also issued
barring Clara from having any contact with
Gail or coming within 200 feet of her home or
office. The judge sternly warned that her bond
would be revoked if she attempted to contact
her late husband's girlfriend.

Clara walked out of the courtroom with her
attorney, George Parnham. When reporters
pressed them for comments, she said her
husband's death was "an accident," but she let her
lawyer do most of the talking for her. She had
selected one of the Houston area's best-known
criminal defense attorneys to represent her.

Replying to a question about the presence of
his client's father-in-law at the hearing, Parnham

told reporters that he thought the Harris family patriarch was there "as basically a tribute to the family entity. He has great empathy for the circumstances. He is a dedicated grandfather to those children and loves his family."

The veteran attorney wasn't inclined to concede any of the accusations or facts outlined in the case against his client and told reporters that he had a lot of investigating to do. "I am not going to discount any aspect until I am thoroughly familiar with what occurred," he declared.

Asked how his client was dealing with the horrendous upheaval in her life, he said she was "just going to try to get her life in order. We have a grieving family. The memory of the father, son and husband is still fresh in everyone's mind," he said. "All parties are going through a very difficult time. I just want to get this young man (David) laid to rest."

Before authorities released the body of the victim for the funeral, another grim and necessary process was carried out. Outside the presence of grieving family, friends, business associates and fellow members of the Shadycrest Baptist Church, David's mangled remains were submitted to an autopsy by pathologists. Forensic pathologists are medical detectives whose job calls on them to solve the mysteries of the dead.

The word "autopsy" is a Greek word that means to see for one's self.

Dr. Dwayne Wolf, Harris County deputy chief medical examiner, conducted the dismal procedure at the medical examiner's office in Houston. The complex, including the morgue, was located at the University of Texas Science Center, Houston campus — where David and Clara studied at the dental school and graduated a little more than a decade earlier.

There in the sterile, cold, matter-of-fact surroundings of death, among the acrid smells of disinfectant, stainless steel dissecting tables, bone saws, scalpels, tweezers and vials, the pathologist and his assistants, dressed in crisp, clean smocks and with white gauze masks over their mouths and noses, gathered around the broken remains.

In most major cities and jurisdictions around the country, autopsies are obligatory for everyone who dies a violent, unnatural or suspicious death. The process is not pretty. Most autopsies begin with the shooting of color photographs of the cadaver. Other pictures are taken at each stage of the procedure. The body is weighed and measured and the autopsy teams make close visual studies of the corpse, carefully recording observations about the location and nature of abnormalities and injuries.

Fingerprints and thumbprints are inked and rolled on cards and samples are taken of blood, urine and other body fluids. Forensic toxicologists later go over the samples, looking for the presence of alcohol and prescription or over-the-counter drugs.

As each sample is collected, they are labeled and slipped into separate containers initialed by the person doing the packaging. From that point on, everyone who handles the samples is expected to sign their own initials or name. Maintaining the chain of evidence is critical and valuable information can be lost to prosecutors — or to the defense — if the chain is broken.

Adult humans have 210 bones in their bodies and in the average male they weigh a total of 12 pounds. David's autopsy disclosed that an inordinate number of his bones were fractured and fragmented. His back, jaw, collarbone, pelvis and 16 ribs were broken. His lungs were punctured and a blood vessel to his heart was torn.

When the scrupulously thorough study of David's remains was concluded, the autopsy report was typed up to become part of the evidence at the trial and then the body of the orthodontist was released to the family for the funeral.

David's life was celebrated and he was laid to

rest during Saturday afternoon services, July 27, in the chapel of the South Park Funeral Home and Cemetery in Pearland. Friends comforted his widow at her home during the difficult hours. She was following the advice of her lawyer and didn't join the mourners at her husband's last rites even though she was free from custody. "The last thing we want to do is create a distraction from the last rites of David Harris," the attorney told reporters.

There were already distractions enough and they seemed to be coming from all directions, greatly increasing the pressure on Parnham's client. One of those distractions led to the first serious courtroom confrontation between the defense and the prosecution.

The prosecution was headed by Assistant District Attorney Mia Magness, a criminal courtroom veteran known for her hard-hitting, in-your-face style of cross examination. She was a tough-minded, capable opponent for the masterly old war-horse at the defense table. Magness recruited help from Dan Rizzo, an experienced, skilled prosecutor who was another of the District Attorney's top guns.

Parnham had filled out his team with defense associates Dee McWilliams, Wendell Odom and Emily Munoz.

With the opposing legal teams in place, there was every reason to believe the approaching courtroom face-off over Clara's fate would be a no-holds-barred humdinger of a brawl and the defendant barely got out the doors of the judicial center with her lawyer after the probable cause hearing before the opening shots were fired.

Magness asked the court to revoke Clara's bond. The feisty prosecutor asserted in the filing that Clara violated the court's order to stay away from her husband's mistress by going to Gail's home early Friday evening, only a little more than 24 hours after her release from jail.

Julie Knight had complained to police that Clara and a man were pounding on the door of Gail's home in Clear Lake about 5:45 p.m. Julie, who was at the house, said she watched while Clara was driven away by her unknown companion in a green SUV. Officer I. H. Franco filed a court document the following day backing up the report about the mystery SUV. He said he saw a vehicle of that description leaving the area while he was driving to the house.

The shocking report appeared to build on an already vivid picture of Clara, in the minds of some, at least, as a blood-crazed hellcat intent on exacting more ghastly retribution on her husband's terror-stricken mistress. It seemed that Gail wasn't even safe while she was holed up in her house with her friend and the kids.

On Monday morning Parnham met with Magness and Judge Davies to sort things out. Clara was meeting with him in his office at 5:45 Friday evening when the two women were seriously spooked by someone pounding on Gail's front door, he said. The woman at the door couldn't possibly have been Clara.

Magness also acknowledged that she talked with witnesses earlier Monday who confirmed that the murder defendant wasn't the woman pounding on Gail's door. The prosecutor withdrew the motion to revoke bond. Clara hadn't violated the judge's order. Some of those involved believed the woman who created all the fuss was a news reporter, but Parnham said he wasn't convinced that anyone at all knocked on Gail's door.

The manner of David's death had clearly left the nerves of a lot of people dangerously frazzled. And the shock, enmity and desire for a balancing of the books by reluctant players in the dark drama were still painfully apparent.

The late orthodontist was in his grave only a couple of days or so before his ex-wife, Debra Shank, filed a lawsuit on behalf of their daughter in U.S. District Court for the Southern District of Texas in Galveston seeking his

estate. Blue Moon wasn't enlisted for any services and one of the agency's competitors, ACTA
Investigations Inc., was hired to serve the court
papers in the case.

Lindsey's mother asked for a restraining
order to freeze the assets and prevent Clara
from spending money from the estate to
defend herself on a murder charge or transfer-
ring money to other accounts. "This court
must act to stop defendant Harris from becoming unjustly enriched by her wrongful acts,"
Mrs. Shank declared in the filing. She said her
daughter, Lindsey, tried to stop Clara, but
"despite her efforts ... was forced to witness the
death of her father." The court issued a temporary restraining order.

The concerned mother also asked the court
to forbid Clara from attempting to contact her
daughter. U.S. District Judge Samuel B. Kent
decided that was something the petitioners
would have to deal with through the Harris
County prosecutors. Soon after that, the case
was transferred to the Galveston County
Probate Court.

A large chunk of David's estate was represented by life insurance. Clara was the sole
beneficiary in three insurance policies totaling
$6.25 million, as well as sole beneficiary in her

late husband's will. But Texas probate and
insurance codes prohibit anyone shown to have
willfully brought about the death of someone
from collecting on that individual's insurance
policy as a beneficiary.

Robert P. Blanchard, another Clear Lake area
orthodontist and lifelong friend of David, was
named executor of the estate. Blanchard had
also taken over operation of the dental clinics.
In September, he was given permission by
Galveston County Probate Judge Gladys
Burwell to file insurance claims for the estate
and pay some of the lenders the Harrises had
borrowed from. One of the smaller policies
named Lindsey as beneficiary, as part of the
divorce agreement between her parents.

According to the executor's petition, David
had one life insurance policy valued at $2.5
million and another worth $1 million, both
with Lincoln Benefit Life Co. He had other
policies with Jefferson Pilot Financial
Insurance Co. and with CAN Life, but the value
was not disclosed in the petition.

A Galveston County Probate Court inventory
of the couple's assets filed about a month after
David's death showed the Harrises had a net
worth of $3.6 million. The couple had accumu-
lated $2.7 million in liabilities, including the

$65,000 still owed on the 2000 Mercedes-Benz Clara used to run her husband down.

Clara's money troubles were worrisome enough, but what promised to be a long, drawn-out contest over the estate was overshadowed by concern about the approaching murder trial.

She needed a lawyer like Parnham, who was widely recognized in the Houston legal community as one of the area's most skillful criminal defense attorneys, because of the seriousness of the charge. Harris County had a reputation for being tough on killers, even by strict Texas standards.

Texas annually executes more convicted murderers than any other state and a modern record was set in 2000 when 39 men and one woman were administered lethal injections. In 2002, the year that David Harris was killed, 33 death row inmates were executed in the Lone Star State.

Harris County is huge, even for Texas, with about one-sixth of the state's population — more than 3 million people — living in 1,800 square miles, an area that's approximately the size of the state of Delaware. The sprawling, big county can usually be counted on to provide about one-third of the state's condemned men and women who walk the legendary last mile in a given year.

Opponents of capital punishment sometimes sarcastically refer to the periodic exercise of the death penalty in the state as "Texecutions." Texans, especially East Texans, aren't bothered by that kind of silly sniping from strangers and continue to apply the death penalty with Old Testament thoroughness and a firm belief in "an eye for an eye."

And despite the shrill claims of noisy critics ranging from Manhattan to Paris, France, and the Vatican, who insist the death penalty is not a deterrent, the murder rate in Harris County is significantly and consistently lower than in comparable urban counties.

Although no women were executed in Texas the year that David was killed, the Lone Star State's legislators, judiciary and juries have also shown they aren't reluctant to strap a female onto the death chamber gurney when she is guilty of an especially heinous crime or series of crimes.

Pretty Karla Faye Tucker, who hacked an ex-lover 20 times with a pickax, then buried the tip of the instrument in the chest of his female companion while she vainly pleaded for her life, was executed in 1998. As her execution date neared, the former prostitute and narcotics addict who turned born-again-Christian in prison became a media darling and poster girl for anti-death penalty forces. She was featured on *Larry King Live*, *Dateline*, *60 Minutes* and other popular shows. Pope John Paul II and Sister Helen Prejean were among religious leaders who unsuccessfully pleaded her case asking for mercy.

The media sweetheart committed the ghastly double murder in 1983 during a robbery to get money for drugs and then boasted that every time she swung the ax she experienced an orgasm. The first woman to be executed in Texas since the Civil War, Karla was put to death with a deadly cocktail of lethal chemicals.

Betty Beets, a mean-tempered barmaid from Gun Barrel City, who disposed of excess husbands under a mock wishing well in the front yard and in a local lake, was executed by lethal injection Feb. 23, 2000. The 62-year-old great-grandmother was so terrified in the final hours before she was strapped to the death chamber gurney that she skipped her last meal. By the time all of her appeals finally ran out, she had spent more than 16 years on death row.

In September 2000, seven months after the Beets execution and nearly two years before David Harris' grisly death, a new 12-cell women's death row was opened at the

Mountain View Unit of the Texas State Prison at Gatesville to replace the old eight-cell facility nearby. Condemned females are driven under heavy guard and secrecy the approximately 75 miles from Gatesville to an all-male prison at Huntsville, where the executions are carried out. The site of a scatter of prisons, Huntsville is about 70 miles north of Houston.

When Clara was charged with killing her husband, there was plenty of room on the expanded death row in Gatesville for new occupants.

Several frightened newcomers, including Darlie Lynn Routier, had already replaced Tucker and Beets on death row in the Mountain View Unit to await their turn in the death chamber. A pretty blond yuppie mother of three from the Dallas suburb of Rowlett, Darlie was convicted in 1997 of brutally stabbing to death her 5-year-old son, Damon. Damon's 6-year-old brother, Devon, was also stabbed to death, but Routier was prosecuted for only one murder.

The experienced lawyer selected to represent Clara was perhaps best known inside and outside the legal community for his spirited defense of another Texas mother from Houston's southern suburbs accused of turning on family members with lethal results. Thirty-six-year-old

Clear Lake homemaker Andrea Pia Yates was charged with capital murder, a charge that provides for a possible death penalty, after systematically drowning her four sons and infant daughter in the family bathtub the previous summer while her husband was at work.

When the last of the children was dead, she picked up the telephone and called her husband, Russell, a computer engineer for NASA, at his office in the Johnson Space Center and advised: "You know, I need you to come home."

The sensational trial ended in March 2002, only three months before David Harris died outside the front entrance of the Nassau Bay Hilton, with a conviction in the deaths of three of the five children. The jury declined to approve death by lethal injection and State District Judge Belinda Hill sentenced Mrs. Yates to a mandatory life in prison.

It wasn't until after the verdict and sentencing that a jurist disclosed on CBS television's *The Early Show* that a couple of her fellow panelists initially voted for typically tough Harris County justice calling for the death penalty. But after jurors talked things over again, they agreed to unanimously support a life sentence. The convicted woman's bearded, white-haired lawyer had waged a spirited defense based on her long

history of postpartum depression, mental illness and suicide attempts.

Like Clara, Mrs. Yates was known as a
privately quiet wife and good Christian mother
who doted on her husband and children. Again
like Clara, she had never before been in trouble
with the law — not even for such a relatively
minor offense as a speeding ticket. And like
Clara, she was once a student at the University
of Texas Health Science Center in Houston. She
earned a bachelor's degree in nursing there.

The two women had much in common and,
until the dour dramas that shattered their lives
were played out, they appeared to be two of the
most unlikely people in the Houston area to
call on a big-time local attorney like Parnham
to defend them in high-profile murder cases.

Reporters were clamoring for more information about the latest Houston-area woman
whose peaceful suburban life as a wife and
mother suddenly collapsed around her feet
amid charges of murder and Parnham said he
was working with her as she tried to get her
emotions in order.

"Something went on within her and she
shares the same need for someone to stand up
and try and articulate what went on in her
mind and with her emotions at that moment,"

he observed of his new client. Parnham said he had already heard several accounts about the lethal events of July 24 and was still working to sort out the conflicting stories.

"Obviously, something triggered what happened. This was not an act that was any way akin to the mentality of Clara Harris," he said. "We have a professional person who is very intelligent."

Then in remarks that some observers theorized may have hinted at his ultimate strategy for defending his client, he said: "When you see the man that you love in the arms of someone else, that has to have such a deep emotional impact on you."

Could it be, various self-appointed pundits, analysts and trial watchers began asking, that the lawyer would mount some variation of a temporary insanity defense? They recalled that a similar defense hadn't worked all that well for Mrs. Yates.

Some of the more experienced and better informed legal groupies even theorized that Parnham might argue "sudden passion" — a defense that when combined with a conviction could lead to a sentence as short as two years in prison or probation. The lawyer said his client would plead not guilty to the murder charge when she was arraigned later in the month, but did not disclose any secrets relating to her planned defense.

While Parnham was mapping out strategy for the battle and grappling with legalities of the case, Clara was busying herself with other matters.

The day she was released from jail, she telephoned Blue Moon and asked for a partial refund of the $1,547.98 paid for the three-day surveillance because the investigation wasn't completed.

Bobbi Bacha told reporters that her former client called about noon and talked for approximately five minutes. Near the end of the discussion, Clara said: "One last thing, you know I paid for Wednesday, Thursday and Friday. I did not get to read your contract whether I was entitled to a cancellation refund."

The experienced private eye responded that the contract makes it clear that if a client appears on the scene of a surveillance like Clara did, no retainers or other money would be refunded.

"And I will tell you why," she declared. "As you found out the hard way, when there is a client on the scene, it jeopardizes our investigators. It jeopardizes the subject. It jeopardizes the client. And so, therefore, there is no refund on this case and we may actually have an additional bill for you because it's going to probably cost us some legal fees and things to go to court."

Blue Moon had another unpleasant surprise for their star-crossed former client. Bobbi told Clara about the videotape shot by their investigator and said it was turned over to police.

"Videotape?" Clara asked.

"Yes, ma'am. We have everything ... but we don't have it in our possession because of the incident that occurred."

Assuming the surveillance was carried out by a man, Clara asked: "So he was there through all the tragic parts?"

"The investigator did video everything because you hired us to video the subject," Bobbi responded. She added that the PI got information of possible adultery because she saw David and his girlfriend going into the hotel.

Clara was still trying to cope with the stunning disclosure that the lethal encounter outside the hotel was captured on film. "There was a videotape?" she asked again. "A videotape of what the tragedy developed?"

Bobbi explained that she didn't know exactly what was on the tape because it had already been turned over to police. Blue Moon Investigations was up to its ears in the complicated tangle and Clara became the key player in the poisonous muddle when she showed up at the surveillance scene and blew her top.

Despite all that and all the other sordid marital messes Bobbi had witnessed in her career as a PI, she was a woman and a wife. Clara was a woman and a fellow human being who was in terrible pain after her storybook life had so suddenly plunged into a chaotic downward spiral. Bobbi offered her sympathy and inquired how the twins were doing.

Clara thanked her. Then she added: "It was really horrible!"

Bobbi audiotaped the telephone conversation and eventually shared the information with the press. She was working on damage control and told reporters that her PI had no idea that Clara was at the hotel during David's surveillance.

"Our investigators have no contact with the client from the field," she said. "In our contract, it says if they show up we will pull off the case." In a printed statement, the company pointed out that its policies prohibited investigators in the field from contacting clients or providing updates on its investigations that were less than one day old.

"Our mission as investigators is to record, document activities and events and collect evidence as such evidence develops, in preparation for court (which we do on all cases to the best of our ability)," the statement continued. "We can never predict or control the actions of anyone."

Blue Moon was cooperating with the Nassau Bay Police Department and had launched its own investigation of events leading up to the tragedy, it was added. But in line with its policy protecting the confidentiality of clients — a policy adhered to by other private detective agencies — the firm made it plain that details of the Harris case would not be publicly divulged without Clara's consent.

In her personal remarks, Bobbi also disclosed to the press that the videotape made by her investigator was turned over to the Nassau Police Department, and stated that it "contain(ed) all of the activities and movements of the subject to the very end." She said that whenever the subject was on foot or in a visible area he or she would be filmed. "If the subject is not on foot we are normally following close behind and listening to conversations."

She declined to publicly provide more specific information about exactly what movement or activities were captured on the videotape.

The detective agency chief's remarks were appreciated by reporters, but they didn't put to rest the curiosity, controversy and criticism that were building over the tapes and over Blue Moon's role in the tragedy.

Blue Moon wanted its material back from police, but the judge gave a thumbs-down on the firm's request and ordered the videotapes handed over to the court and placed under judicial seal.

Thousands of dollars were also reportedly offered by some media outlets for copies of the tantalizing tapes. But the judge's firm action short-circuited any chance that the media would be inflaming the passions or influencing the thoughts of prospective jurors or of anyone else by showing the taped images on nightly news broadcasts. And print reporters wouldn't be describing them in any publications, at least until the information was disclosed at trial or the judicial seal was removed for some other reason.

For the time being, the tapes were even off-limits to Clara's defense team and they wouldn't be allowed to take a look at them and at other prosecution evidence until after their client was indicted by a grand jury — if then. A request from Parnham for copies of all audio and videotapes linked to the death of his client's husband was firmly rejected by the judge. It wasn't even certain at that point if the tapes would be accepted as evidence at the trial, a decision still to be made by the judge.

That didn't stop the defense lawyer from citing interviews with witnesses that led him to theorize the mysterious videotapes might turn out to be more helpful to his client than to the prosecution. "I believe if the tape is clear," he said, trying to put a positive spin on the evidence, "then it could only support my belief about what happened in that parking lot."

CHAPTER 9

Daddy's in Heaven

W hen Clara returned home from jail she told the twins that their father was on a business trip. But their routine was so disrupted that they seemed to realize something in their lives had changed forever. They wanted to know when Daddy was coming home and she didn't have an answer for them. Finally, Mom told the kids their father would never be coming home. Brian stunned his mother with another question.

"Is he in Heaven?" the child asked.

In a brief interview with NBC's *Today*, Clara said she couldn't believe that the twins immediately understood.

While Clara was endeavoring to cope with the twins and the ghastly turn her life had taken, her family and friends rallied protectively around her. Most, except for members of the immediate Harris family, were unaware there was serious trouble in her marriage until they heard the dreadful news of David's death and of her arrest on charges of murder.

Between the time David confessed the illicit affair to his wife and the night he was killed, everything simply happened too fast. There was no time for her to sit down with a trusted girlfriend and pour her heart out over her troubles or seek helpful advice.

Three of her closest friends, Shelly Canada, Amy Redus and Gina Blanchard, were eventually interviewed on CNN's *Connie Chung Tonight* show, broadcast from New York.

Canada, Clara's longtime chum whom she first met at the Texas Medical Center, said that immediately after learning of the disastrous confrontation at the hotel she wrote a touching letter to her friend. Clara told her she read the letter from time to time to keep her strength up.

But Clara wasn't the type to run to other people with her problems because she was the one who was always concerned about others, her fellow dentist said. Canada explained that she and her friends had to drag information out of Clara because "she was in a daze" and couldn't believe what had happened. All she had wanted to do was keep her husband. "They were a team," Canada declared. "This was the love of her life. She never wanted to hurt him. Never!"

Canada also theorized that Clara's discovery that so many people among her immediate circle of friends knew about the affair before she did may have been a factor in leading her to hesitate before going to one of them for help.

Redus and Blanchard were also supportive and said they talked with their friend after David's death.

Redus first met Clara 10 years earlier through the Shadycrest Baptist Church, which they attended along with David and the elder Harrises. Redus said she believed Clara when she described David's death as an accident.

Blanchard was less forthcoming than her companions and although she said she had known Clara for 11 years and talked with her after David's death, she couldn't remember details. But Clara "felt terrible about the whole thing," she recalled.

Reverend Steven Daily, the Shadycrest pastor, along with his family and most or all of the church's congregation, strongly supported the distressed woman and prayed for her. Clara was a faithful and generous member of Daily's flock and a few years earlier she approached the clergyman and advised him that she had decided to provide free dental care for his family of five.

Clara's mother was crushed when she heard the terrible news that David was dead and her brilliant, loving daughter was accused of killing him. The heartbroken woman wanted to fly to Texas to be with her daughter during the crisis in her life and support her during the ordeal of the trial. But the old woman was in such frail health that Clara wouldn't consider it, especially because she didn't know if she would be free for very long to help handle her mother's medical needs. Two male cousins from Colombia were already living and working in the Houston area and they were among the first to rally to her support.

Surprisingly, in what would become one of the most bizarre elements of the case, three of Clara's most ardent and loyal supporters were David's parents, Gerald and Mildred Harris, and David's psychologist brother, Gerald Jr. An aunt and uncle also stepped up to support their late nephew's widow. Described as a decision of "love" and "Christian compassion," some of the family's neighbors in East Texas found this difficult to comprehend.

The Harris family support of Clara also created an agonizing rift with Lindsey, who couldn't reconcile her relatives' backing of the woman she watched run down and kill her father with a car.

David died a gruesome death and the domestic tragedy generated by the seamy love triangle was pounced on by the press and quickly became international news. The story was ready-made for newspapers and the electronic media and had all the elements necessary to boost circulation and ratings.

There was a self-absorbed, philandering husband, a long-suffering wife turned homicidal, a mistress depicted as a predatory home-wrecker and a ghastly, bloody death that was about as public as it could be.

Furthermore, the poisonously lethal drama was played out against a lurid backdrop of failed marriages, bitter divorces and accusations of a scandalous lesbian affair in the neat upscale yuppie enclaves scattered around south suburban Houston and the Johnson Space Center. It was a salaciously strange story that was perfect for the media — and for late-night television talk-show hosts who had a field day making jokes about the terrible event of July 24.

The hometown *Houston Chronicle*, nearby Galveston's *Daily News*, Houston's Channel 2 and other local television stations, gave the story prominent daily coverage. But the story also garnered headlines throughout the country and around the world. The Big Apple's boldly brassy daily tabloid, the *New York Post*, headlined a story, "Mad Wife At Wheel." An English tabloid described Clara as the "Driller Killer."

Former employees, friends of Clara and others who had at some time in their lives come into contact with them were swept up in the morbid fallout from the star-crossed couple's sudden sinister celebrity. It seemed that anyone who had ever said "hello" to Clara or passed her on the street was suddenly appearing on television to tell their story and recount their personal experiences with the notorious woman who made such a public spectacle of running down and killing her husband with her expensive luxury sedan.

Even Parnham submitted to an interview with Paula Zahn on CNN. "Who knows what happens to a loving wife, obviously a loving mother, a person who wanted to maintain the sanctity of the union with her husband, when unexpectedly, she is confronted with the picture and the reality of the very fine man that she loves in an embrace with another female?" he asked.

In addition to talking with NBC's *Today*, Clara taped her own interview with CBS television, but airing of the show was withheld until after her trial. She told the interviewer that David said he thought he loved both her and his mistress.

The media clamor became so intense that Parnham hired a public relations firm to handle the deluge of requests for interviews and information about his client, his plans for her defense and the upcoming trial.

"I'm astounded by the attention," he confessed. "It's greater than Yates. I think it's the sensationalism of the situation."

The prosecutors, who worked for a district attorney's office that handled about 260 murder cases annually, said the case would be given no special treatment as far as the media was concerned. Magness declared that she was treating the Harris case just as she would treat any other murder case she handled for the county. She predicted there would be no surprises at the trial, but suggested, "some people's perceptions may be altered."

The lavish home (above) Clara and David Harris (right) shared before their dream marriage turned sour.

Gail Bridges (left), David's mistress, and Julie Knight (right) appear in disguise on the Sally Jessy Raphael show. Their husbands hired a private investigator in an attempt to uncover a suspected lesbian love affair.

Death Car – the Mercedes sedan (above) Clara used to run over her husband in the parking lot of the Nassau Bay Hilton Inn (left). David Harris was helping his mistress Gail Bridges into her Lincoln Navigator (below) when his enraged wife gunned the engine of her car and ran him over. Years earlier, David and Clara had held their wedding reception at the same hotel.

Clara Harris leaves the courtroom during her murder trial flanked by Mildred and Gerald Harris. David's parents initially supported Clara, citing "Christian compassion."

Gerald Harris Jr. (left), David's brother, joins his parents in testifying for the defense. Witness Evangelos Smiros (right) describes how the victim's body flew through the air after being struck the first time by the Mercedes.

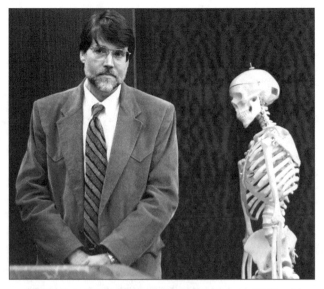

Harris County medical examiner Dr. Dwayne Wolf said that David's back, jaw, collarbone, pelvis and 16 ribs were broken after being run over.

Expert accident reconstructionist Steve Irwin, speaking for the defense, speculated that David had only been hit once by his wife. Multiple eyewitnesses who saw the victim being run over repeatedly disputed his findings during the trial.

"Take him to the cleaners ... Get his house, car, kids — but you don't get to kill him," argued prosecutor Mia Magness during closing arguments (right).

Judge Carol Davies (right) watches over the proceedings in the 177th State District Court in Houston, Texas.

Lindsey Harris (above right) leaves the court with her mother, Debra Shank (above left) after the teenager's gutwrenching testimony. Lindsey was in the front passenger seat when her stepmother ran over her father.

Witness John Tyler (left) demonstrates how David Harris pulled his wife off of his lover as the two women fought viciously in the lobby of the Hilton hotel. Clara attacked Gail Bridges as she and David emerged from an elevator following their final tryst.

Running out of gas — Clara testifies in her own defense. "All this happened in a fraction of a second," said the accused. "I didn't have time to think."

*Clara Harris is supported by her attorneys,
Emily Munoz and George Parnham, after being
found guilty of murder in the death of her husband,
David Harris. Judge Davies sentenced Clara to 20
years in the Mountain View Prison in Gatesville, Texas.*

Those perceptions were still being formed and hotly debated in the comfortably affluent communities where the Harrises had lived and tended to their dental patients. Gossip and rumors were rampant wherever people got together in the workplace, in restaurants and bars and salons.

People just couldn't keep from talking about the case. Talk radio hosts helped fan the flames and newspapers were filled with letters to the editor, taking one side or the other. For weeks, every talking head doing local news or commentary on the tube had something exciting and new to report or a personal observation to be passed on to viewers.

It was clear that for many people the tragedy struck an emotional chord that was intensely personal. Observations ranged from the righteous to the wickedly vengeful and all three of the people who played leading roles in the deadly melodrama — Clara, David and Gail — were selected by various commentators to shoulder the lion's share of the blame.

Several observers who expressed their opinion in the public forum concluded that David signed his own death warrant when he threw his outrageous two-timing in the face of his wife, then allowed himself to be caught redhanded with his mistress.

As "the other woman," Gail was given a solid
working over and some women preceded their
opinions with vivid descriptions of their own
troubles with "homewreckers" and deceitful
females on the prowl for vulnerable husbands
who could be lured away from their wives with
promises of sex and romance.

Clara was also roundly castigated, most often
by men, and depicted as a vengeful wife whose
blood lust wasn't satisfied until she killed her
unfaithful husband. Much of the malicious
blather circulating throughout East Texas after
the bloody showdown inside and outside the
Nassau Bay Hilton was wild speculation or the
result of too many witnesses with too many
versions of what they thought they had seen.
Every police detective, criminal defense lawyer,
prosecutor and judge knows that eyewitnesses
taken by surprise and reacting with shock to
unexpected or especially grisly events can be
notoriously unreliable.

One of the most common bits of misinforma-
tion spread through the gossip, and some early
press reports, indicated that Clara ended the violent rampage at the hotel by parking the heavy
Mercedes on top of her husband's body. Those
reports were quickly proven to be mistaken.

The defense and the prosecution were also

taking close looks at the number of times the heavy car circled the median and rolled over the body of the victim — or as some courthouse wags put it, how many "victory laps" Clara made around the track. The conclusions were expected to play a prominent role in the upcoming trial.

As pre-trial maneuvering was stepped up and the final courtroom showdown neared, there was strong speculation in the local legal community that Clara would be convicted of murder and her attorney would wind up making a last-ditch effort to win her freedom by convincing a jury to settle on probation because she acted in "sudden passion." Parnham further fueled the speculation when he remarked: "The burden is on the state to establish a rational state of mind at the time of the act. I absolutely believe she did not intend to kill him."

In most instances, a good defense lawyer plays it close to the vest and doesn't give away his game plan before the trial. But if fellow lawyers haunting the corridors and the courtrooms of the Harris County Judicial Center were making bets, they would have likely put their money on Parnham following through on that belief and arguing that his client didn't know what she was doing and didn't mean to kill her husband when she mowed him down.

Parnham predicted that the Harris couple's relationship would take center stage. "And it's absolutely true that had David Harris been a faithful husband," the lawyer declared, "he'd be here today with his family." In additional remarks he provided hints that backed up speculation he would attempt to paint Clara as a saint, while depicting her husband and his girlfriend as the villains.

"It's a woman scorned case, bottom line," Parnham declared. "Her whole married life, her future with her husband, raising those two boys was jeopardized when those elevator doors opened and David Harris and Gail Bridges walked out. God knows what goes through a woman's mind when that happens!"

The mind of another troubled woman who was a key player in the tragedy was also cluttered with violent images, worry over the future and concern for her children.

When *Texas Monthly* headlined the investigative piece in its November edition, many people following the case learned for the first time that Gail and her chum, Julie, had appeared in disguise on television's *The Sally Jessy Raphael Show.*

Despite the absence of any definitive evidence supporting the accusations of lesbianism, gossip about the sexual practices of the two female friends was already rampant. The latest revelation poured more fuel on the fire. Local TV outlets began broadcasting sound bites from the show. The *Houston Chronicle* published a picture of Gail in her wig and dark glasses taken when she appeared on the show. And the *New York Post* jumped back into the picture with a story printed under the lurid headline, "Bisexual Triangle Led to Car Slay of Hubby."

If having her private life exposed and surgically examined by hordes of strangers was difficult for Clara, it was also devastating for David's battered mistress. Already scorned and berated as a homewrecker, she was further maligned as a sexual deviant; a modern-day Hester Prynne — with an invisible scarlet letter "L" on her forehead, as well as an "A." People turned away or whispered about her when she shopped, accompanied her children at school functions or attended church.

Gail didn't go much of anywhere for a while after the terrible night at the Hilton when her lover was run down and killed. Her mother reportedly cared for her while she recuperated from her injuries and the emotional trauma. "Gail is quite traumatized," attorney Valerie Davenport observed of her client's friend.

Gail discouraged news reporters from pounding on her door by lowering her window shades and posting signs along the driveway and sidewalk in front of the house warning against trespassing. That didn't stop professional and amateur photographers from hesitating in front of the two-story brick home and shooting still pictures or an occasional videotape.

She also hired a big-time Houston attorney, Dick DeGuerin, to help look out for her welfare. It was a move that was certain to attract even more headlines and attention from the press. Publicity was something the celebrated 63-year-old Texas lawyer was used to — and apparently welcomed.

He made international headlines in 1993 when he shouldered his way into the deadly siege of the Branch Davidian compound near Waco. The colorful lawyer was hired by the mother of cult leader David Koresh to represent her son and he boldly rode through police lines and up to the L-shaped compound known as Ranch Apocalypse on a motorcycle. He eventually made several trips inside in an attempt to bring a peaceful solution to the crisis and to explore the cultist's legal options.

DeGuerin's gritty efforts to save lives ended in failure when U.S. Attorney General Janet Reno ordered federal forces to attack and they launched an assault with armored combat vehicles and CS gas. Ranch Apocalypse burned to the ground, killing more than 80 cultists, including women and children who were inside.

The attorney wouldn't have to pilot a motorcycle to see his new client and Gail wasn't being put in peril by an army of heavily armed FBI and Bureau of Alcohol, Tobacco and Firearms agents. But the tensions and strain on she and on her friend, Julie, were agonizing

The new mess that Gail had gotten herself into lacerated and ripped open the still festering wounds from the brutally corrosive divorces she and Julie had undergone and the bitterly fought contests over custody of their children. Both ex-husbands went back to family court in Galveston and filed to reopen the custody cases stemming from their divorces.

In his petition, Steve Bridges cited fears that his children might be in danger because of enmity toward Gail on Clara's part. He asked for exclusive custody of all three of the couple's children.

"According to what my ex-wife has told me, Mrs. Harris savagely attacked her in the lobby of the hotel and ripped her shirt off," he declared in the court document.

Steve said in the filing that while Gail worked for David, she and the children socialized with the family of her employer. "Both Gail and I are very concerned because Mrs. Harris knows our children," he declared. "Gail has told me she feels that her life is in danger." He added that his ex-wife believed Clara was "initially aiming for her with her Mercedes and she indeed struck the Navigator before she struck Dr. Harris."

Gail was upset over the media attention and had been contacted by a reporter about the allegations of an affair with Julie, forcing her into hiding, he said. Steve also claimed she was currently living with Julie and their relationship was "a stormy and sometimes violent one." Just a few months ago his daughter had to call 911 to police to break up a fight between the two women at Gail's house, he asserted.

Steve also claimed Gail took an overdose of pills in 2000 in a suicide attempt, but survived because she made herself throw up. (She has denied ever attempting suicide or using illegal drugs during their marriage.)

"I know there are many people in the Clear Lake area who believe that my ex-wife and Julie Knight had a romantic relationship even as I assume my ex-wife and Julie Knight will deny those allegations," he declared. The message was clear. In the estimation of Gail's ex-husband, the children were not living in a safe or proper environment.

Chuck Knight responded to the hullabaloo over his ex-wife's pal by also seeking full custody of his children. He said he was worried that as long as his ex-wife continued her close friendship with Gail that the children could be endangered if Clara came around looking for the woman whose romance with David had led to such terrible trouble.

"In my opinion, since the murder of Dr. Harris, it is not in the best interest of my children to reside with their mother or to be in her possession at this time," Chuck declared in his petition.

Julie quickly struck back through her lawyer, who lashed out in support of both her client and her client's friend. Defending Gail, Davenport described her as a woman who was physically injured in the scrap at the hotel and was in love with David and still grieving his death.

"She's devastated," the lawyer said. "She saw the man she loved run down. This man told her he was leaving his wife and getting a divorce."

The scrappy attorney told reporters that accusations of lesbianism against the women were all false, but they were ruinous to the children involved. The nastiness had caused some organizations to shun the Knight children, she said. They were reputedly told by local leaders of a national youth organization not to come back, "because we don't condone homosexuality."

In a statement that might have been seen in some quarters as supporting the fathers' concern, Davenport added that people were "banging on the doors" and the children were terrified.

"These are old accusations known not to be true in an effort to capitalize on tragedy," Davenport said of Chuck's filing. "I'm going to move for a temporary restraining order to shut this stuff up."

Davenport also accused Gail's ex-husband of feeding the media frenzy with false allegations about lesbianism and firmly denied that the two women were living together.

She criticized Steve as a controlling husband who had tried to dictate the kind of lipstick his wife wore and even made her wear makeup when she was in bed with the flu. "He said her breasts were too small and her backside was too big. He ridiculed her in front of everyone," the lawyer declared.

"Even when a detective agency could find no evidence of a lesbian relationship, he throws it out there and makes his kids watch TV coverage of it."

Chuck filed for his own temporary restraining

order, asking the court to prohibit Gail from having contact with his children. The petitions and motions were scheduled for a hearing in the 306th District Court of Judge Susan Baker in Galveston.

When Gail and Julie showed up for the hearings, the mob scene in front of the courthouse made it look like the Academy Awards had been moved to East Texas. The women could barely force their way through the scandal-crazed media crowd to get into the courthouse.

Once inside, the women had reached a temporary sanctuary and relief from the press that was extended a short time later with a clampdown on information by the judge. Baker sealed the files and instructed attorneys not to talk with reporters about anything that went on in the hearing.

Dee McWilliams, one of Clara's attorneys, was among the gaggle of lawyers who trooped into the courtroom. Gail's lawyers had asked him to attend. While carefully avoiding discussion of anything that occurred inside, McWilliams told reporters during brief remarks on the courthouse steps following the hearing that his client wasn't a threat to anyone.

Shortly after his wife and her friend made their court appearance, Chuck dropped his petition. Steve continued to seek full custody of his kids.

CHAPTER 10

Pre-trial

On Wednesday, Oct. 9, a Harris County grand jury returned an indictment charging Clara with the murder of her husband by running him down with her silver Mercedes. The indictment read in part:

"The Defendant, heretofore on or about July 24, 2002, did then and there unlawfully, intentionally and knowingly cause the death of

David Harris, hereinafter called the Complainant, and did cause the death of the Complainant by intentionally and knowingly committing an act clearly dangerous to human life, namely, striking the Complainant with a motor vehicle." The indictment was signed by the grand jury foreman, whose name was blocked out in printed copies.

Like much of the procedure in American courtrooms, the practice of keeping grand jury proceedings and the identity of members of the panel secret evolved from English law. It was developed in the old days as a tool to protect grand jurors from the Crown.

King Henry II came up with the idea for the original grand jury, but he used it in 12th century England to get at his enemies and to levy taxes. Initially it was known as an "accusing jury" because the panel was ordered to name criminal suspects. The more named, the better, because grand jurors — who were often called "informers" — could be fined if they didn't finger enough suspects.

People unlucky enough to be named by a grand jury were often fined if they admitted to their reputedly dishonest ways. Others often had to submit to trial by ordeal and prove their innocence by holding a burning iron in their bare hand without dropping it, float in a pool of water while both hands were tied behind their back without drowning or survive other tortures designed to elicit a confession.

In the early days of the United States, the grand jury was also frequently abused, but the move to secrecy was a major factor in reforming and reshaping the system and turning it into a legitimate and effective tool for law enforcement.

In America today, shielding the identity of members of the panel and of witnesses who testify before it is considered essential to the grand jury's ability to function properly. The defendant does not appear before the grand jury and is not represented by an attorney. The prosecution leads the jury through the case. He, or she, is not required to reveal all the evidence, just enough to justify the return of an indictment.

When the grand jury met in Houston to consider the role played by Clara Harris in the death of her husband, the indictment was no surprise to her or to her defense. Parnham announced that his client would enter a not guilty plea at her next court appearance on Oct. 18. "I am convinced that she did not intend to in any way hurt or harm, or much less take the life of her husband," he declared.

There hadn't been much to brighten Clara's life since she learned of her husband's philandering, but the indictment was actually good news, because the charge of murder — rather than capital murder — had once and for all ruled out any possibility that she would face a possible death penalty. Murder was the same offense specified in the preliminary charges filed against her.

According to Texas law, murder is considered a capital offense only if one of several special circumstances are involved. Those circumstances include such aggravating conditions as a slaying that occurs during commission of another crime such as armed robbery, rape or other offenses; hiring a killer; killing a child under age 6; the murder of a firefighter or police officer, and other special factors.

Although Clara would never be locked up with the other women in the new female death row at Gatesville, she could face spending the rest of her life in prison if convicted of the most serious charges against her. Even with the possible charge of capital murder taken off the plate, Parnham was faced with a daunting task if he expected to win freedom for his client so she could return to the half-million-dollar family home in the Polly Ranch Estates subdivision to mother her twin boys and rebuild her life.

There was a time in the memory of older Texans when the law was much more tolerant of crimes of passion. But even then, the odds were stacked heavily in favor of men who snapped and committed murder after finding that their spouse was cheating. A law enacted in 1925 and known as the Paramour Statute stated that homicide was justifiable if a husband caught his wife in flagrante delicto. But the aggrieved husband was justified only in killing the lover, not the wife.

Three important factors would have prevented Clara's legal team from basing her defense on the old Paramour Statute, even if the case had gone to trial in 1925, according to legal scholars.

First, she was a woman and the old statute was written to benefit husbands who caught their wives playing around. Secondly, even if the statute had applied to wives as the aggrieved parties, she would have been bound by the same restriction that permitted only the killing of the lover, not the spouse. Finally, even killing the lover wasn't considered justified unless the adulterers were caught in the act.

Clara didn't catch her straying husband and his mistress in bed together in their sixth-floor hotel room. She confronted them as they walked out of the elevator into the hotel lobby

— and at that time they were doing nothing more intimate than holding hands.

The loophole at one time provided by the Paramour Statute for crimes of passion was narrowed considerably when the criminal codes were changed to define slayings of that type as voluntary manslaughter.

In 1994 voluntary manslaughter was wiped off the books and replaced in the Texas State Criminal Codes with the current stipulated offense of murder. But like voluntary manslaughter, conviction on the new charge of murder allowed juries to consider "sudden passion" as a mitigating factor during sentencing. That was an important provision for Clara, because if she was convicted of murder without the mitigating factor, she could face a possible penalty of life in prison.

If Clara had been charged with the same crime in one of several other states, her defense might have chosen to argue temporary insanity in an effort to win an acquittal or leniency for their client. But Texas law makes no provisions for a plea or finding of temporary insanity and if she was convicted of murder, arguing "sudden passion" in the penalty phase of her trial could be the next best thing.

Three factors must exist to justify a finding of

sudden passion as legally defined in Texas criminal codes. Those factors must include evidence to show the accused was provoked by the victim or by someone with him or her; the provocation made an ordinary person so enraged that he or she was incapable of cool reflection, and the crime occurred at the time of the provocation.

At her arraignment before Judge Davies on Friday, Oct. 18, Clara formally entered the anticipated plea of not guilty to the murder charges.

Parnham groused at the hearing that he still hadn't been given a look at the now-famous videotape and other evidence he needed for the defense of his client.

Rizzo responded that the defense had already received more than it was entitled to and added that the material was provided earlier than ordered by the court. "We're continuing to give them full access to almost every file that we have with the exception of some work Friday," he said. Judge Davies ordered all evidence the defense was entitled to see to be provided by the following Friday.

Parnham spoke briefly to reporters after the courtroom jousting. "There's a mental aspect here," he said about his client's thinking processes and emotional state on the night of her husband's death. "Every facet of her life will be relevant to her mind-set on the 24th. Today was simply going through some housekeeping procedures and letting the court know what's happening as far as discovery is concerned. We've got a lot of work to do and we're in the process of trying to get through it."

Jury selection for Clara's trial was scheduled to begin Tuesday morning, Jan. 21, 2003, in the 177th District Court at the Harris County Criminal Justice Center in downtown Houston. Months earlier the attorneys and the judge had met in Davies' chambers to set the case schedule and agreed to move the trial into the early days of the following year so there would be time for both sides to pull together the complicated facts.

Parnham later told the press that he believed the prosecution was making every effort to ensure that it had all the facts and pointed to the early erroneous reports that his client left her car parked on top of her husband's body the night he died.

"It seemed to be a callous act on her part and we know that's not true," the lawyer said of the stories. "I think the prosecutor's office, in all fairness, wants to make sure an accurate representation is made."

Dressed conservatively in a neat business suit
and with her hair darkened, Clara quietly
watched from the spectator's gallery while the
attorneys returned to the courtroom and
formally set the case schedule. She didn't speak
in court or to reporters outside after the
proceedings ended. She would turn 45 years
old on Jan. 3, less than three weeks before the
beginning of the trial that would determine
how she would spend a big chunk of the rest
of her life.

Old wounds were reopened on another front
when a complaint was filed with the Texas
Commission on Private Security against the
detective agency that was up to its neck in
the courtroom maneuverings and intrigues
surrounding the increasingly complicated case.
The state commission launched a probe of Blue
Moon, but refused to publicly disclose details
of the investigation.

News reporters told Bobbi Bacha about the
complaint before she was notified by the state
and she theorized that it stemmed from a disagreement with a Nassau Bay police officer and
had nothing to do with the activities of Blue
Moon investigators. Bobbi said the detective
agency sent a letter to Nassau Bay police complaining that one of their officers made false

and misleading comments to a television news crew the day after David's death.

"The reporter asked if our investigators led Clara Harris to her husband and she (the officer) said 'pretty much,'" Bobbi said. " 'I thought, 'Oh, my God.' "

Reporters were in for a surprise when they followed up on their talk with Bobbi by asking Nassau Bay Police Chief Ron Wrobleski about the complaint. He said it wasn't filed by anyone associated with his department.

Wrobleski explained that one of his officers was contacted by an investigator with the commission and asked for information a few days after the events at the Hilton. Another Nassau Bay police officer telephoned the commission to confirm the investigator's credentials and was told that the first caller was indeed instructed by supervisors in Austin to make an inquiry. Wrobleski added that his internal affairs division was investigating the complaint against his officer detailed in the letter from Blue Moon.

Newshawks had to look somewhere else to track down the originator of the complaint to the state commission, but close-mouthed bureaucrats refused to identify the individual who filed it or to provide other details until their probe was complete. When the media continued the quest to find the complainant, reporters were led to Chuck Knight. But Julie's ex-husband didn't respond to their efforts to contact him by telephone.

Once Bobbi learned where the complaint originated, she had a lot to say to reporters. The complaint was groundless and motivated by Chuck's personal anger at the firm, she declared. And it didn't have any direct involvement with the death of David Harris. Blue Moon agents testified in Chuck's divorce and he lost money, Bobbi pointed out. Blue Moon also testified in his girlfriend's divorce and she lost custody of her children. "So he doesn't like us very much," the PI chief said.

While Bobbi was defending Blue Moon's role in the case and filling in the press on Chuck's perceived motivations for filing the complaint, preliminary maneuvering was nearing a conclusion in preparation for the trial.

A deposition from Lindsey was disclosed by Magness in a hearing, quoting the girl as saying her stepmother told her, "I could kill him and get away with it for all he's put me through." Clara made the damaging remark about an hour before she struck her husband and ran over him with the car, according to the statement made under oath but outside the courtroom.

According to the assistant DA, Lindsey also told prosecutors that just before Clara drove her car into her husband, she said, "I'm going to hit him."

The statement in Lindsey's deposition was later used to draw a big laugh from the audience during the appearance by Clara's friends on *Connie Chung Tonight*. Canada was asked by the show's hostess if it was true, as Lindsey said, that Clara declared, "I could kill him and get away with it."

"Connie," Canada replied, "I've said that about my husband so many times."

There was nothing laughable to Parnham about the statement. The defense attorney wasn't permitted by the teenager's attorneys to speak with the girl and he asked the judge to suppress the damaging deposition disclosed at the hearing and keep the statements out of the trial.

Davies ruled against the motion, but tossed a bone to the defense by barring the prosecution from referring to Lindsey's remarks in opening statements. That wasn't even a half-victory for Parnham and he worried that the statements would taint the jury.

"The horse is out of the barn unsaddled," he complained after the deposition was read at the hearing. "The jury will have heard them. It is extremely unfair to Clara Harris." The lawyer claimed the statement was taken out of context and firmly denied his client ever said she was going to hit her husband with the car.

The defense attorney lost another preliminary skirmish when Judge Davies told him he would not be allowed to refer to the reputed lesbian relationship between Gail and Julie. Parnham had argued that the question of lesbianism was tied to the relationship of the parties involved and was important to the case, regardless of how inflammatory it might be.

Sometime around the year-end holidays, one more weird incident in an already bizarre case occurred. Burglars broke into the new offices of Space Center Orthodontics at 1140 Clear Lake City Blvd. and stole Gail's employment file. The office was only a short drive or a long walk from the former Space Center Orthodontics offices at 2323 Clear Lake City Blvd., where David and Gail had worked together and begun their disastrous affair.

The burglary in the building David was planning to move into before his death was discovered on Sunday, Dec. 29, by a cleaning crew. The cleaners notified police after noticing that a computer and two 27-inch television sets were missing. Three window screens were damaged. The office had been tidied up last on Dec. 22, when nothing was out of place. The office was closed during Christmas week.

When employees were recruited by police investigators to check other office furnishings and equipment, it was determined that two video game systems, a couple of computer trays and a single personnel file — Gail's — were also missing. It was extremely unlikely that the file could have been selected by accident from so many others.

But why would someone want the file bad enough to break into the new office building to get it, investigators wondered? And were the other items stolen to cover up the real objective of the burglary or were they hauled away simply because it was convenient since the thief was already inside?

As author Lewis Carroll quoted his young heroine as saying in *Alice In Wonderland*, things were becoming "curiouser and curiouser."

After months marked by a flutter of motions, briefs and other legal filings by attorneys on opposing sides, most of the loose ends were at last tied up. Chinks, loopholes and exceptions to the Texas Criminal Codes, judicial rules and high court opinions had been thoroughly explored and debated. Frustrating hairsplitting

arguments over admissible evidence and other
murky legal loggerheads were also ironed out
— if not to the satisfaction of the opposing
teams of lawyers, more importantly, to the satisfaction of the judge.

One of the more contentious debates ended
with a decision by Judge Davies that the dead
man's behavior could not be used by the
defense in "an effort to establish his bad or
questionable character."

She also forbade the defense from making
any mention to the panel indicating that
David's family supported an acquittal, conviction on a lesser offense, a probated sentence or
minimal incarceration for Clara.

But the judge said she would allow Parnham
to inform jurors of Clara's behavior in the frantic
week leading up to her husband's death, including her decision of improving her physical
appearance with breast augmentation surgery.

Friends and employees of the Harris' and witnesses to the terrible events of July 24 had been
interviewed by police, the prosecution and the
defense. Some were interviewed twice or more.

In compliance with the process of discovery,
evidence gathered by police and prosecutors
had been shared with the defense. There would
be no "Perry Mason" surprises in the courtroom

to suddenly tip the trial one way or another. Perry Mason was fiction — Parnham, Magness and their colleagues were real trial lawyers.

At the last moment, Parnham made one final announcement — Clara would testify in her own defense. "She realizes her life and the lives of her children hang in the balance," he told reporters. "She continues to express sorrow for being the cause of her husband's death. The acceptance of her testimony by the jury will be crucial."

The lawyers were ready, the legal justice system was cranked up and the stage was set.

Early Tuesday morning, Jan. 21, jury selection began in the 19th floor courtroom of State District Judge Davies.

The local, national and international press were allocated 50 highly coveted seats for the media event about to take place in the Houston courtroom. Reporters or producers for the *CBS Early Show, Good Morning America* and Court TV were among the leaders of the pack and settled in to cover the entire trial along with their brothers and sisters of the press from Houston and other major Texas cities.

One pool sketch artist, one pool still camera and one pool television camera were allowed inside the courtroom. But television reporters and backup technicians were advised they would be permitted only to record video images and were banned from broadcasting sound during testimony. No audiotape recording devices or other cameras would be allowed.

The judge made an exception to the no-audio rule and said she would allow television crews to broadcast sound during opening statements.

Strict rules of behavior were also imposed on reporters, camera operators and various broadcast technicians, all of whom were warned that any disruption of the courtroom proceedings would result in the removal of the offender, his or her equipment — and possibly all media equipment from the courtroom. Depending on the circumstances and severity of the offense, journalists could also be cited for contempt.

No-nonsense Judge Davies ran her courtroom like she was a captain of a ship. She didn't make the law, but she laid down the rules about the conditions under which it would be carried out in her courtroom.

One of the restrictions banned the media from taking still pictures or videos of any citizen called by the court to participate in selection of the jury.

Only a few days before jury selection in the Harris case was set to begin, the role of the media in Texas courtrooms made news when the Texas Court of Criminal Appeals heard arguments in a case involving the decision of another Houston judge who agreed to allow the PBS documentary series, *Frontline* to tape jury deliberations in the death penalty trial of an accused carjack killer.

Prosecutors appealed the decision of State District Judge Ted Poe, arguing that it would result in violation of jury confidentiality. The judge's attorneys responded that cameras could shed valuable light on the process of capital punishment. The appeals court did not indicate when it would come up with a ruling.

Judge Davies had already put a tight rein on the press before Clara took her place beside her attorneys at the defense table for the beginning of voir dire, the examination of the members of the jury pool. The defendant was dressed in a neat business suit, her usual courtroom wear, as the process got under way to pick members of the panel of fellow citizens who would decide her fate.

Wearing the simple gold wedding band David had given her almost 11 years earlier, she was escorted into the courtroom by her husband's parents, Gerald and Mildred Harris. It was a procedure they would follow faithfully every day of the trial. They sat quietly behind her with other family members as an expression of their love and support for their son's widow and the mother of their twin grandsons.

"We are the proud parents of David and Clara Harris and the proud grandparents of Lindsey and Brian and Bradley," Gerald Harris told reporters outside the justice center. "We are a close, loving Christian family. Our ultimate hope in all of this is that this family will remain together as a strong family and that our grandchildren will have their parents. We love Clara and want you to know that we want her to be with her children."

Clara retained custody of the boys while she was on bail and their paternal grandparents were frequent visitors to the mansion in the gated Polly Ranch Estates.

Months earlier, Gerald Harris had described the behavior of both his son and his daughter-in-law as being tragically mistaken, but said they were both fine people. He then provided all the insight that was needed into the motivations of himself, his wife and other relatives who supported Clara by observing that if God could forgive the sins and mistakes of His children, then it was good and proper for the Harrises to forgive the sins and mistakes of others.

The loyalty and love of the Harris family was

seen as commendable and courageous by some, but difficult to comprehend and accept by others. The family's unwavering and wholehearted support for the woman who killed their son would be commented on and debated throughout the trial and long after it was concluded.

Inside the Justice Center, as Judge Davies began the process by questioning each one of 120 men and women called for the jury pool, there were no disruptions or violations of the rules by the media. She made sure of that by banishing the press to another room where they watched the jury members' examinations via a wide-screen television.

Not everyone summoned as part of the pool were happy campers and some would clearly have liked to beg off from their duty as citizens to sit through an anticipated two- or three-week trial. They preferred to read about it or to get their information the easy way from radio or television, if they were interested at all in the case.

Other court authorities had already weeded out the convicted felons, noncitizens, the genuinely ill or disabled and others with legitimate reasons for skipping jury duty. When it was Judge Davies' turn to ask questions, the prospective panelists learned that she wasn't someone who could be easily fooled or cajoled into giving someone a walk. She had been around too long to fall for "my dog ate my homework" stories or complaints about being too important to take time off from a job. If prospects were eliminated by the judge, it would be for other reasons.

Judge Davies didn't react favorably to a request by Parnham to include more Hispanic women in the pool of potential jurors to sit in judgment of his Colombia-born client. If Parnham had expected to gain some kind of advantage by beefing up the Hispanic representation on the panel, his hopes were dashed. The move was firmly rejected.

Judge Davies culled nearly 50 prospects early Tuesday, before turning questioning of the remaining 72 over to the prosecution. Magness asked each prospect if he or she thought David's death was a result of "sudden passion."

The prosecution explained that in order to find that someone committed a crime of sudden passion, the person had to be provoked by the victim at the time of the offense. The actions of the victim also must have caused anger, rage, resentment or terror in someone who was "of ordinary temper," sufficient to render the mind incapable of cool reflection. Eleven of the prospects replied that they believed sudden passion was involved with Clara's action and two of those survived to be seated on the final jury panel.

Like the prosecutor, when it was Parnham's turn at bat he grilled members of the jury pool on their own romantic relationships and marital experiences. He also asked if they believed his client was "guilty of something" and about a quarter of the pool replied in the affirmative.

Only one of those, a woman who had said she believed David's death resulted from "sudden passion" and also conceded that she could "emotionally relate" to the defendant, was picked as a juror. Earlier she also said she was concerned about the possibility of being sequestered because she had a premature baby. Another woman, when asked if she could emotionally relate to the defendant, responded that, "Any married woman can." She was struck from the pool later in the procedure. A man who said he thought "anyone would be sympathetic" was also passed over.

Other prospects were struck from the pool because they had already formed an opinion that Clara was guilty, were biased for the defense and for various other reasons. The judge barred some from the panel after being asked by the defense or prosecution to eliminate them for "cause" because their views in the case appeared to be in conflict with the law or they had opinions that would prevent them from rendering a fair judgment.

Many of those questioned confirmed hearing reports or reading stories about the case at least five times. Three other people ultimately selected for the jury or as alternates also conceded they read or heard about the case five or more times.

Both the prosecution and the defense also used their peremptory right to strike as many as 10 prospects each for any reason except race or sex.

By late Tuesday afternoon the defense and prosecution had settled on a jury of nine women and three men. Two women were named as alternates. Clara's fate would be determined by a panel of jurors who had admitted to a divergence of attitudes going into the trial. Two jurors and both alternates knew someone who had been murdered or otherwise died violently. One juror was selected even though she reported that she had significant medical problems.

With the exhausting but vital process behind him, Parnham observed:

"I think we have a thoughtful, thinking, compassionate jury that can understand what she was going through on July 24. There were a number of people that could identify with Clara Harris. Certainly we welcome that only because we think the evidence will support issues that women, in particular, but women and thoughtful men can understand and take on."

The heavily lopsided female makeup of the panel led to a challenge from the prosecution, but the motion was denied by Judge Davies. The prosecution took the setback in stride and Rizzo later said of the jurors: "They look like a real fair group of people, so we're real happy."

The work of the defense and of the prosecution was clearly cut out for them and it seemed that neither side could make any conclusions ahead of time about a certain or easy victory — or of a bitter defeat. The trial was expected to last at least two weeks.

number of the Harris County Criminal Cra...

CHAPTER 11

The trial

The State of Texas

V.

Clara L. Harris, Defendant

A gaudy circus poster advertising a performance by some modern-day Buffalo Bill Cody
Wild West Show couldn't have had more
sensational impact than the simple statement
at the center of the event about to begin on the
19th floor of the Harris County Criminal
Justice Center. The Justice Center is a busy
place every day of the workweek, but activity

was especially intense on Wednesday morning, Jan. 22, as attorneys prepared to deliver opening statements in Clara's murder trial.

Just outside the imposing structure with its sterile corridors and hushed atmosphere, a couple of earnest young men with scraggly long hair shoved leaflets into the hands of strangers. Professionally printed, some of the leaflets read:

"Whoremongers and Adulterers God Will Judge" Hebrews, Xiii, 4

Others ominously warned:

"The Land is Full of Adulterers" Jeremiah, Xxiii, 10

Most of those who accepted the fliers glanced at them amused and then absentmindedly crumpled them into balls and dropped them into a nearby trash receptacle. A few people folded the fliers and slipped them into an inside jacket pocket, a briefcase or a purse.

Inside the grim stone building, crowds of lawyers, court employees and run-of-the-mill citizens jostled with fringe members of the media passed over in the allotment of seats in efforts to find space in the courtroom.

There was something about a woman, a wife and mother, charged with carrying out or planning the violent death of another human being that fascinated and captured the imagination.

The sensational trials a few years earlier of
Wanda Holloway, the so-called "cheerleader hit
mom," fed on the same kind of morbid allure.
The obsessive mother from Houston's eastern
suburb of Channelview captured headlines for
nearly 10 years during two trials for putting out
a hit on her neighbor and former best friend.

Wanda was obsessed with seeing her daughter, Shanna, win a highly coveted spot on the
cheerleading team at the Alice Johnson Junior
High School. But Shanna was edged out the
first year of tryouts by other girls, including
the daughter of her neighbor, a former varsity
cheerleader. The second year of tryouts,
Shanna was barred from competition, reportedly
because of her mother's meddling.

So Wanda decided to step in and assure a win
for her daughter in her final year at Alice
Johnson Junior High by arranging a hit on the
mother of the neighbor girl. Wanda reputedly
figured that the young cheerleader would be so
upset by her mother's death that she would
blow the tryouts. But the would-be hit man
wasn't comfortable with the idea of rubbing
out the mother of a 13- or 14-year-old girl and
he set Wanda up for an arrest.

She was convicted of solicitation to murder
during one of Houston's most sensational trials

and sentenced to a 15-year prison term. Unfortunately, so many inconsistencies were uncovered, including a juror who was on probation for a felony, that a judge declared a mistrial and Wanda was freed.

Convicted at a second trial that was as melodramatic as the first, Wanda was again sent away to prison, this time for a 10-year term. But she behaved herself inside the walls and was freed after serving only about six months, including time served before the mistrial was called.

Clara Harris, whose destructive act was widely described as the "Murder by Mercedes" case, was the latest suburban Houston wife and mother to be making national news during a high-profile homicide trial.

Judging by snippets of conversation inside and outside the courtroom, there was a visible element of class envy involved in the massive public captivation with the case against the former Lake Jackson dentist. By the standards of the Houston area's large working class population, Clara and her husband were fabulously wealthy. It didn't matter if it was old money or new money, there was a certain satisfaction on the part of some who were less blessed with wealth in watching the rich get their comeuppance.

That was especially so when a modern-day

Pandora had lifted the lid off a box full of yuppie demons that revealed a blanket of sores festering with accusations of sexual perversion, back alley romances and the use of a sleek, expensive foreign car as a killing machine.

Students from the Baylor University Medical School and David and Clara Harris' old alma mater at the University of Texas Health Science Center mingled in the spectator seats with oil well drillers, secretaries and soccer moms for whispered debates about the guilt or innocence of the defendant and to speculate on the court-room tactics of the prosecution and defense.

A resident in neurosurgery who took time off to watch the trial wondered at "the fine line between sanity and madness." A woman who snagged one of the last open seats in the spectator section was barely settled in before she leaned over and confided to a neighbor that during a quarrel over her husband's drinking, she once shoved him into a pool, knowing full well he couldn't swim.

As they did at preliminary hearings and during the jury selection process, David's parents escorted their daughter-in-law into the courthouse. They wore badges identifying them as members of the defense and occupied seats set aside for the family just behind the defense table.

After Judge Davies disposed of a few motions, the prosecution at last began to outline its case against the defendant. In American jury trials the prosecution goes first. Clara "turned her $70,000 vehicle into a 4,000-pound murder weapon," Magness told the jury. "The evidence will show you she intentionally and knowingly hit him and didn't stop. She did it again and again and again." After pleading for a final dinner, supposedly to break off all ties with his girlfriend, David still wasn't really sure which woman he would choose, the prosecutor said. Clara was obsessed with hanging on to her husband, didn't trust him to keep his promise to end the relationship and so she hired a private detective agency to "get some dirt" on his girlfriend. Magness cautioned jurors that they should expect to hear the defense try to paint Clara "as the victim" and to "do what they can to dirty up David Harris."

When the angry wife gave her husband an ultimatum at the hotel and he chose Gail, Clara got into her car and decided to run him down, the prosecutor said. "Clara Harris got mad. She intentionally and knowingly hit David Harris with her vehicle and he died as a result. And the bottom line, folks, is that's murder!"

During the defense's presentation, Parnham depicted Clara as a loving mother and devoted wife. She only wanted her husband to come home and was heartbroken after finding out he misled her and refused to end the affair, the lawyer declared. Clara softly sobbed and wiped at her eyes as her attorney told the jury that she was a woman who was only seeking to keep her family together, then " loses it" after surprising her straying husband with his mistress at the same hotel where they were married.

"The elevator door opens and out steps David and Gail Thompson Bridges," the lawyer declared. "David comes over, a martial arts aficionado, pulls his wife and throws her to the floor."

The defense attorney presented Clara to the jury sympathetically as a woman who acted in the heat of anger and betrayal. Parnham said she didn't even realize what she had done until she got out of her car, then seeing her husband on the pavement she lay on top of the dying man, crying, "David, David, David, I'm sorry."

On the morning of David's death he swore to his wife that he would end the affair, the lawyer told the rapt jury, "Clara was overjoyed. It had been a horrific week. She knows she will be able to keep her husband and keep her family intact." But instead of keeping his word, David arranged a tryst with his mistress that evening, Parnham continued.

He said that when his client discovered the lovers at the hotel, she wanted to stop them from leaving together. Defining Clara's state of mind, he described her thoughts as: "Gail Bridges cannot have my husband. I want him home. I want to take him home with me."

Parnham told the jurors they would hear testimony about what happened just outside the hotel but asked that they reserve judgment until they heard evidence "about what physically happened in that parking lot ... whether or not Clara Harris intentionally caused the death of David Harris."

As testimony opened in the prosecution's case, Evangelos Smiros was called to the witness stand and recounted the dreadful scene at the Nassau Bay Hilton. The hotel food and beverage director recalled hearing David yell at his wife, "It's over! It's over!"

"If looks could kill," Smiros said of Clara's reaction, "it sent shivers through me." Minutes later "she peeled rubber." The witness told the jury he watched helplessly as Clara struck her husband with the car, then ran over him three times. Those words struck at the heart of the defense contention that David's death was an accident and he was run over no more than once.

Parnham grilled Smiros and other witnesses

who testified that Clara repeatedly ran over her husband with the silver sedan — one claimed as many as five times — pressing them to back up their statements with precise recall. Four witnesses, all hotel employees, eventually conceded that they couldn't be sure how many times David was run over.

Smiros also described Lindsey's unsuccessful efforts to get out of the speeding car. She was unable to get out until it was finally braked to a stop. Then she yelled at her stepmother, "You killed my dad," he said. "I never thought in a million years she would do something like this, nobody thought that," Smiros said of the defendant.

Paul Garrett Clark recounted the catfight between the two women in the hotel lobby and said he watched as Clara was "pulling and screaming" at Gail. "She punched her with her closed fist in the face, knocked her to the ground and then punched her in the face again," he said of Clara's furious assault. While the women were mixing it up, David didn't intervene.

"Gail was a mess afterward," Clark continued. "She was upset and scared for her life, shaking, trembling. She couldn't complete a sentence." The witness then recounted escorting the shaken woman outside to her car, while the orthodontist trailed behind them. Moments later he was brushed by the speeding Mercedes, then watched helplessly as it plowed into David.

"I heard loud automotive noises, acceleration, along with cackling. I saw the accused driving her vehicle toward me. I looked up at David. He had bulging eyes, a terrified look. He was facing the oncoming Mercedes," the young hotel employee vividly recounted. "The defendant hit David and came to a complete stop. He flew about 25 to 30 feet." Clark added that Clara drove in circles, running over the body three or four times, then reversed and ran over him again.

Parnham began cross-examination by questioning the witness about inconsistencies in his testimony, compared to statements he made to Nassau Bay Police about an hour after the incident. He struck especially hard at Clark's remarks that Clara was "cackling" and statements to police that she continued to scream and laugh while bearing down on the victim in the Mercedes. Under the spirited verbal assault, the young hotel clerk backtracked. He conceded that he didn't remember the defendant "cackling" and said he only heard screaming.

Jose Miranda, a night manager at the hotel, gave testimony similar to Clark's — without the references to cackling that got Parnham's dander up. "I couldn't believe I was seeing this after I saw the first hit," he declared.

Early on the second day of testimony, the defense was rocked back on its heels with a bombshell remark from Robert Williams, the Conroe diesel technician who rushed to the mortally injured man from the hotel pool after hearing the commotion in the parking lot.

Williams quoted Clara as telling her dying husband: "Now you see! You see what I can do!"

The statement was dramatic, damaging and apparently hadn't been made earlier to police. It wasn't recorded on any of the documents filed during the pre-trial maneuvering and was a total surprise to the defense team.

The shocking remark also struck solidly at the defense contentions that David's death was an accident and Clara wasn't in her right mind when she plowed into him with her car.

Parnham didn't waste time getting to the heart of the matter when he moved in for cross-examination. "Your statement you made on the stand — that's pretty powerful, wouldn't you agree?" he asked. Williams agreed.

"That's a statement that goes right to the heart of this case," Parnham continued, while indicating his surprise that there was no written record of the remarks. "This is the first time you've ever told anybody anything along these lines?"

Again the witness agreed. He hadn't told anyone about the statement before, not even his fiancée, Julie Creger. Williams said he hadn't discussed the case with her, but conceded that he overheard her when she was giving her statement to police.

Creger followed her boyfriend to the stand, telling her own story of trying to help the badly mangled man and to keep him breathing. Both witnesses provided the jury with grisly descriptions of the dying man, who was bleeding profusely, struggling desperately to breathe and was unresponsive to those trying to help him.

Creger burst into tears as she emotionally recounted her effort to unclench David's teeth and open an airway. "His breath was terribly labored. It was a wet breath. He gasped deeply, his chest sounded congested," the witness said. "I started to hold his hand and told him, 'You need to keep breathing.' "

She also told of walking Lindsey away from the body and asking her, "Who did this?"

Several jurors turned from the witness to peer at the defendant when Creger quoted the teenager's reply: "My mom, I mean my step-mom." Clara slumped in her chair and dabbed at her eyes with a handkerchief as the witness told about asking if the woman had meant to do it, then quoted the teenager's affirmative reply.

After his fiancée was excused from the witness stand, Williams came up with his second surprise of the day. He asked to return to the stand so he could clarify some of his earlier testimony. After he was sworn in once more, he strongly defended his earlier testimony about the surprise statement he attributed to the defendant about showing her husband what she could do. But he ran into trouble when he tried to explain why he hadn't mentioned it earlier. Williams asserted that he didn't know Magness was with the district attorney's office, and explained that was why he hadn't brought up the contentious statement before.

Parnham pounced on the opening. He asked Williams to produce the subpoena calling him as a witness. Williams pulled out the subpoena. Magness was clearly named on the document as an assistant district attorney.

Williams also drew a few titters from spectators when he defined his earlier statement on the stand that he didn't drink alcohol. The diesel mechanic admitted he had a bourbon and Coke the night David was killed, but said he didn't consider that to be drinking.

The witness's return to the stand appeared to have been a mistake on his part. It damaged his credibility and cast doubt on his previous testimony.

Two women who were attending a real estate seminar at the hotel when they became reluctant witnesses to the disastrous confrontation also testified.

Heidi Hendrick said she was walking to her car when she heard the angry verbal exchange between the Harrises. Clara had a "possessed look" when her husband yelled repeatedly that their marriage was over, she told the jury. "She seemed stunned and proceeded to scurry off to the car with her daughter. She peeled out of the parking space."

Norma Ramos testified that she saw Clara screaming to everyone around her in the lobby that her husband was having an affair with his receptionist. "They had direct eye contact. He even tried to get closer to her. He pointed at her and said, "This is over. No more. It has ended. You have to realize it's over," the witness declared. "And she didn't say anything." As the Harrises argued, Lindsey sat on the ground crying, Ramos added.

Asked by Parnham during cross-examination if David attempted to comfort his distraught daughter, Ramos replied: "He looked down at her, then looked at Mrs. Harris. Without saying anything, he walked toward Gail Bridges' car."

Friday afternoon the jury finally got a look at the highly guarded videotape filmed by Lindsey Dubec. It was a big disappointment to a lot of people who had expected it to be the smoking gun that would show the defendant's Mercedes slamming into the victim, then circling the grassy median and repeatedly bumping over his limp body.

The tape shot from inside Dubec's car was grainy and fuzzy and didn't show much more than a few seconds of images of a big car with its lights on making tight, quick circles in the hotel parking lot before coming to a stop behind a bush. The young PI hadn't even begun to roll the film until after David was run down.

The film began with the camera zooming in and out showing momentary images of different cars in the parking lot, including David's and Gail's. Clara's luxury sedan was already in motion when it first appeared on the film and only two-and-a-half more circles of the lot were shown. The video did not show the car being driven in reverse over David's body as Clark had testified.

The film was out of focus and the distance it was shot from and the darkness of the evening despite lights in the parking lot and at the hotel entrance, all had an effect on its poor quality. About the only thing that was really clear was that the film was not shot by a professional photographer.

Images of the Mercedes appearing to go up and over something could be vaguely made out, but it was unclear what the object was. As the film flickered faintly, Magness pointed to a white object near a bush and told the jury it was David's body. From seats in the spectators' section, and probably from the vantage point of the jury box, it was hard to tell.

Clara covered her face with her hands while the short two-minute tape was played by prosecutors and shown on a television screen in the darkened courtroom. Only about 30 seconds of the film focused on the actual event, but she was so distraught by the time the television set was finally clicked off that Judge Davies called a five-minute recess so family members could comfort her and calm her down.

Although it may have seemed doubtful to many disappointed observers that it would do much to help or hurt either side, Parnham interpreted the film as supporting the case of the defense.

"The jury had already heard about the going

around in circles of the Mercedes. It seems to me it was descriptive of the chain of events that contradicted much of the eyewitness testimony," he told reporters. "We saw no reversal. We saw no back-and-forth. And to that extent I think it was helpful."

In accordance with their custom, neither of the co-prosecutors, Magness and Rizzo, shared their views of the proceedings with the press after court was adjourned.

When testimony resumed, Dubec, who was no longer employed by Blue Moon, told the jury about trailing David to the hotel and observing his meeting with his girlfriend. She testified about grabbing her camera and shooting the film after hearing the commotion, watching people spill out of the lobby and recognizing David and Gail. Her chum who came along to keep her company on the stakeout became so hysterical after witnessing the grisly events that Dubec had to drive her home before returning to the hotel as quickly as she could and identifying herself to police as a witness, the former PI added.

Dubec conceded that she initially told police she went into the hotel and saw the lovers together, but admitted under questioning that it was really her friend who went inside.

Although she didn't capture the entire incident with her camera, the witness declared that she knew what happened to David that night — he was run over with a car.

During cross-examination, Parnham asked if other witnesses would be needed to verify that. "Right ... I didn't see it," Dubec responded.

When court was adjourned for the weekend break, no one could have been more relieved than the defendant. After listening to the grisly testimony describing her husband's injuries, reluctantly reliving their violent final confrontation and watching the grainy film made of her Mercedes circling the median strip in front of the hotel, Clara was in torment. In the words of her lead attorney, she was an "emotional wreck and a bundle of nerves."

The prospects for the resumption of testimony when court resumed on Monday morning didn't promise any relief. After a weekend at home with the twins, Clara was smartly dressed as usual and appeared composed while she was escorted into theJustice Center by her in-laws for the beginning of the second week of her trial.

Claudine Phillips, the PI supervisor, was one of the first witnesses called and told of her conversations with Clara at the offices of Blue Moon Investigations. Phillips described the defendant as being "very professional, composed, straightforward" in her belief that her husband's mistress was attempting to manipulate him to her own advantage.

"You could tell she really loved her husband. He was a good man who had fallen into a trap," Phillips testified. "She said that over and over again." Clara blamed herself for making it easy for her rival and was regretful for devoting more time and energy to caring for the twin boys than she spent with David, the witness said. "She felt she had opened the door to this woman to steal her husband."

The proceedings turned particularly gruesome Monday afternoon and Clara once more had to struggle to maintain her composure when Magness began introducing evidence to show the blood and gore at the crime scene to jurors. Photographs of blood pools and spots in the parking lot, telltale dents in the shiny Mercedes, a shock of artificial hair from David's prized toupee and the tooth that fell out of his mouth were all admitted as evidence.

On Tuesday morning when the prosecution introduced graphic autopsy photos of David's hideous injuries accompanied by testimony from the pathologist who conducted his autopsy, Clara lost the tenuous composure she had maintained during the previous day's exhausting ordeal. And she wept silently during testimony about finding chunks of hair, grass and a big smear of blood on the undercarriage of the Mercedes.

Detective Julio Cesar Rincones of the Webster Police Department testified about David's blood, palm prints and fingerprints found on the defendant's silver sedan. One palm print was lifted from a spot near the hood ornament and another near the driver's side fender.

During Rincones' testimony the windshield wiper blades ripped from Gail's SUV and photographs showing the deep scratch marks inflicted when Clara keyed her rival's vehicle were introduced as evidence. Although Rincones said he couldn't lift fingerprints from the broken wiper blades, Parnham conceded that his client committed the vandalism.

Parnham grilled Rincones during cross-examination about personal items found in the Mercedes and identified a wedding album the detective had referred to as a photo album. The lawyer asked Rincones if he preserved the wedding album as evidence.

Rincones replied that he hadn't considered the album to be relevant and didn't keep it or mark it as evidence. "I guess it's still in the car," he said. Parnham asked the judge to subpoena the wedding album as evidence.

Dr. Dwayne Wolf had taken the witness stand and was about to explain that 16 of the victim's ribs were fractured and the splintered bones punctured internal organs, when the defendant broke out into loud sobs. She pitched forward with her elbows propped on the defense table and her head buried in her arms. Her shoulders shook and she wailed uncontrollably while members of the defense team hovered over her and attempted to help her regain control of her emotions.

Judge Davies reacted immediately to reprimand the defendant. "We're not going to have any outbursts during testimony," the jurist sternly declared.

Despite the judge's admonition, Clara continued to wail. For the moment, at least, getting her to quiet down was a doomed effort and Parnham conceded the defense team's lack of success. "I don't know how we're going to do that, your honor," he told the judge. "If she's going to cry, she's going to cry."

Judge Davies finally called a 15-minute recess to give the defendant an opportunity to bring her emotions under control and Clara's attorneys led her unsteadily from the courtroom.

Clara had regained temporary control of her sobbing when she returned with her attorneys and again took her place at the defense table. Parnham was sincerely trying to comply with Davies' orders and promised the judge that he would approach the bench at the first sign that his client was losing her composure again.

As the witness resumed testimony, Clara nevertheless dabbed at tears and burst into loud new fits of crying that continued intermittently throughout the remainder of the day. Even though she was forewarned and had a good idea of what to expect, her emotions were frayed and shattered, and telling her to stop crying was like telling the rain to go away.

Dr. Wolf had barely begun again to detail the catastrophic skeletal and internal injuries to the victim when the defendant began to loudly sob once more.

Judge Davies was becoming increasingly annoyed by the repeated disruptions and she let Parnham know she was peeved. Peering down from the bench and fixing him with an icy stare, she declared: "The defendant is audibly weeping. I can hear her and the jury can hear her."

Parnham knew everything he needed to know about arguing a motion, examining or cross-examining a witness or filing an appeal — but he didn't know how to turn off the tears when a heartbroken woman was sobbing uncontrollably.

"I understand," he pleaded with the judge. "Believe me, I want this not to occur." Parnham blamed his client's behavior on the agony of hearing her husband's injuries so graphically described, made all the worse when she was accused of being the person responsible.

Magness was no more forgiving of the defendant's loss of control than was the judge. It wasn't fair that jurors were not listening to prosecution testimony because they were being distracted by the sobbing of the defendant and the patting and comforting efforts of the defense team, she complained.

"If the defendant cannot sit quietly, I will remove her from the courtroom," Judge Davies threatened while fixing Clara with a disapproving eye. "I don't want to do it, but I will. It's your choice." The judge didn't have a reputation for bluffing.

"I'll stay here, I'll stay here," Clara blubbered in words that were barely intelligible through her tears.

Judge Davies was determined to get her point across and further admonished: "You will stay quiet and not react, as difficult as that may be."

Clara tried to explain why she was having so

much difficulty controlling her emotions. "Your Honor, it's the first time I've heard what's happening," she sniffled, her voice quivering.

With the question of courtroom interruptions hopefully settled, the painful queries about David's injuries started all over again. Wolf testified that a photo of David's body showed a leg injury consistent with a car running over him. The victim was run over at least twice, he said.

At one point, as Magness was questioning the witness, McWilliams broke in and said the defense would stipulate that the victim was struck by an automobile and run over. Clara was still having a hard time handling the grisly testimony.

When it was the defense's turn to ask the questions, McWilliams conducted an aggressive cross-examination and consistently attacked the experienced pathologist's conclusion that the victim was run over at least twice. Recalling that a police officer had already testified that the Mercedes cleared the ground by only about six inches, the defense attorney suggested to Wolf that some of the injuries may have been caused by dragging. He asked if it was possible that the injuries could have been caused by a car passing over the body only once.

"There were four wheels and he was twisting and turning when he was run over," the attorney began.

An experienced witness, the pathologist shut him off with a quick correction. "There were four wheels and he may have been twisting and turning," Wolf said. The emphasis was on the words "may have been."

McWilliams tried again. "Assume scientific evidence showed that he was struck once, carried and rolled over," he suggested.

Wolf was satisfied with his previously stated conclusions and he made that clear to the defense attorney. "If that's what the autopsy indicated, that's what I would have testified," he said. "I don't see this pattern of injuries fitting the scenario you're describing."

As agonizing and draining as testimony had already been for the defendant, there was worse to come. Clara's stepdaughter, Lindsey, had been widely described in the press as "the star witness" who could make the difference between a conviction or an acquittal.

One prominent Houston lawyer who sat in on the trial confided to reporters that "everything could rise or fall on that poor little girl's testimony." Many other observers from the local legal community agreed.

The teenager, who turned 17 in January, began her testimony Wednesday morning. Magness gently led her through the events of the previous summer that culminated with the dreadful death of her father in the parking lot outside the front entrance to the hotel. Lindsey told the jury that after arriving at her father's home for her summer visit she noticed a dramatic change in the relationship between him and his wife. Clara often slept with the twins instead of in the master bedroom with her husband, the girl testified.

While working at Space Center Orthodontics, she noticed her father and his new receptionist flirting with each other. When she saw him affectionately place his hand on his receptionist's leg she became even more suspicious that something wrong was going on, she said. After recounting her father's confession to his wife of an affair and of Gail's firing, Lindsey told about pleading with him to behave himself. "I thought the affair was wrong," she said, "but I still loved my dad."

Lindsey described the frenzied search for her father on the evening of July 24 after Clara became suspicious that he hadn't broken off his affair with his mistress as promised. The girl said she rode along because she wanted to comfort her stepmother.

"She was on a mission to find where he was

— she was determined," Lindsey declared. "They had tricked her. They had hidden from her and she was upset by that."

Until Clara became aware of the dangerous rift in her marriage, she had less time for her stepdaughter than she had during previous visits. The emotional support provided by the high school cheerleader for her troubled stepmother seemed to be bringing them closer together again, according to Lindsey's testimony. She was becoming her stepmother's trusted confidante.

But the dynamics between the girl and the woman she had once called "mom" were forever changed by the violence that cost David Harris his life. The young witness was no longer Clara's confidante — or friend. And she drove another nail solidly into the coffin of the defense contention that the death was an accident when she described a chilling statement by her stepmother.

"She said she could kill my father for what he had done and get away with it," Lindsey testified. "She was calm and I didn't think anything of it. I knew she wouldn't do anything like that."

Lindsey said that she could tell her stepmother was enraged and her face was red when they got into the Mercedes following the brawl in the lobby. "She had an evil expression on her face," the girl testified. "We backed out — fast!"

Turning to the final minutes of her father's life, Lindsey quoted her stepmother as saying, "I'm going to hit him."

"She was very determined that's what was going to happen," the teenager said. "I screamed 'No!' lots of times. But she stomped on the accelerator and went straight for him.

"He was really scared. He was trying to get away and he couldn't."

After striking David, Clara circled around and struck him twice more, never making an effort to avoid him, the young witness added. "I was really upset and was screaming, 'You're killing him!' " Lindsey said she tried to get out of the car but her stepmother was driving too fast.

"I could tell the difference of the bump when we went over a big cement curb and when we went over my dad," she said.

No one on the jury uttered a sound and the awful statement from the mouth of the young girl hung over the courtroom like a dark shroud, evoking a horrible mind's-eye vision of Lindsey trapped in the front seat of the speeding Mercedes and forced to watch through the windshield while her father's body was crushed and mangled by the heavy car. Some jurors leaned forward in their seats as Lindsey talked, totally absorbed in the heartrending account. The girl maintained her composure while testifying, although at times her voice quivered and she appeared to be fighting back tears.

"I knew she had killed my dad," Lindsey declared. "She said, 'I'm so sorry. I'm so sorry. It was an accident. Are you OK?' "

Lindsey didn't believe her father's death was an accident and she made her feelings crystal clear to the jury. "It wasn't an accident. She knew what she did," the teenager bitterly went on "And she wasn't sorry!"

The statement rolled through the silenced courtroom like a thunderclap. It created a picture of an act that was premeditated — the absolute opposite of an accident.

Clara was quiet and covered her face with her hands during much of the painful recitation about the hours leading up to the lethal confrontation and about the confrontation itself that ended with David fatally injured. But her self-control broke down again and she began bawling when the teenager described her father's gruesome end.

This time Judge Davies left Clara in the courtroom and sent the jury out when she called an adjournment. She was fed up with the disruptions and gave Clara an ultimatum.

"Either you will sit here in a composed manner or you will be removed from the courtroom," she said. "Is that understood?"

Tears smeared Clara's mascara and streaked down her face as she replied in a tiny voice that was part whimper, part whisper that she understood. Wiping at her eyes, she took a deep breath and sat up straight in her chair, seemingly determined to tough it out. The jury was summoned back into the courtroom.

Parnham conducted the cross-examination and he handled the fragile witness with kid gloves. He turned in a good performance the previous week by chipping away at the testimony of eyewitnesses to the fatal encounter outside the Nassau Bay Hilton. But Lindsey was no Dr. Dwayne Wolf or Robert Williams, grownups who had witnessed horrible things but were light years away from enduring the magnitude of the personal trauma experienced by the slender girl who was testifying.

It was evident to anyone in the courtroom that the pitiful teenager was emotionally scarred by the appalling events she was forced to witness on the moist East Texas summer night when her father was killed. It was no time for a defense lawyer to be confrontational.

Under the experienced lawyer's ginger

questioning, Lindsey confirmed that a wrong-ful death suit was filed on her behalf against her stepmother.

Lindsey blamed the love affair partly on her stepmother's lack of attention to her father. But she said she told him not to leave her step-mother for the other woman. She described Gail as a fake and "the personification of evil."

When the Columbus, Ohio, high school student at last stepped down from the witness stand after a grueling near five-hour ordeal, it was clear the defense had taken some hard hits.

Even then, Lindsey wasn't through for the day. She stood quietly by the side of her step-father, Jim Shank, and let him do the talking when he spoke out against the defendant during a statement to a gaggle of reporters on the courthouse steps.

"We've heard a lot about Clara Harris and how hard this has been on her," Shank told the assembled journalists. "However, the focus should be on Lindsey and how hard it has been on her brothers and family. This has been a very trying time for all involved and we are trying as a family to get our lives back to some semblance of normalcy. We will not be satisfied until justice is served. It does not matter how angry you get. You do not have the right to kill anyone for any reason, especially in front of an innocent child."

The protective stepfather didn't comment about Parnham's suggestion that the wrongful death lawsuit filed on Lindsey's behalf might have influenced her testimony.

Parnham also talked with reporters after court adjourned for the day and said he was surprised by Lindsey's performance on the witness stand. "In direct examination, she came across embracing Gail and her father, putting it off on Clara for spending too much time with the twins," he said.

Some other courtroom observers didn't share the lead defense attorney's surprise. In pre-trial filings, Lindsey had already made it plain who she blamed for her father's death. There was no getting around it, Lindsey's testimony was dramatic and heartrending — and from all appearances it could only help the prosecution in its quest to convict her stepmother of murder.

The wily defense veteran had one or two witnesses of his own lined up that he was counting on to help turn the tide in Clara's favor. One was the woman named as the home-wrecking mistress of the dead man and she was expected to be called as a hostile witness.

The other, more doubtful witness was the

defendant. Clara was eager to testify, but the defense hadn't yet made a hard, firm decision about calling her to the stand.

But that was a few days in the future — the defense had other witnesses to call first as they began to present their case to the jury on Friday for their client's acquittal.

After Lindsey's poignant testimony, Judge Davies took time out to deal with defense plans to call an accident specialist to the witness stand and present two films including a high-tech animated video to the jury. The animated video was designed to simulate the path the Mercedes took before running over the victim. The hearing took all day Thursday and was conducted without the jury present while Steve Irwin of Dallas outlined his qualifications as an accident expert and told the court that after investigating, he concluded that David was run over only once.

The expert said he was prepared to testify that the vehicle was traveling 15 to 20 mph when it struck the victim, then circled around him three times without hitting him again. It was "more probable than not" that David's body was carried some distance on the hood of the Mercedes before being hurled to the pavement, he said.

Irwin had assembled a large array of exhibits to back up his planned testimony, including the animated video re-creation and the other video, which he described as a live "drive-through" tracing the path of the Mercedes. A vehicle similar to Clara's was used for the drive-through.

Magness mounted a strong argument against showing the videos to the jury. "If the videos showed what the defendant saw, there wouldn't be a fuss," she complained. "It purports to be evidence supporting their theory, but it's not accurate." The assistant district attorney also said she was concerned that the appeal of video presentations could cause the jury to give more credibility to them than they deserved and that could come at the expense of more reliable oral testimony.

Judge Davies ruled that Irwin could be called as an expert witness, but the defense couldn't show either of the videos to the jury. She said she wasn't sure about their reliability. The judge also pointed out that the animated film didn't show the pedestrian who was struck and the drive-through misrepresented speed and the perspective of the driver. The vehicle traveled slowly and the camera mounted in the center of the car didn't properly represent the viewpoint of the driver, she said.

Although they still had their witness, loss of the videos was a huge disappointment for the defense. Odom had referred to them as part of the "guts of defensive thought in this case."

The defense may have been gutted, but Parnham and his team hadn't suffered a mortal blow. "Our expert will just have to work harder," the lawyer told assembled reporters after the hearing.

Friday morning, Irwin was called as the first defense witness and although he was barred from using the videos, he was still armed with a dazzling array of computer-generated charts and maps. He told the jury that David couldn't have been killed in the manner the prosecution claimed. Although Clara drove her heavy car in tight circles around her husband's crumpled body, she didn't repeatedly run over him, he said. David was run over only once.

"If you get in this car and make a turn and rocket left you can never get back to that mark," he said. Irwin was relating his discussion of the luxury car's turning radius to blood spots on the pavement where David's body landed after he was struck and hurled through the air.

A civil engineer especially trained to analyze traffic accidents, the confident witness declared that he inspected skid marks and other evidence to reconstruct the speed and the route of the Mercedes, while factoring in its turning radius. He said the heavy luxury sedan could turn in circles no more tightly compressed than 40 feet. The accident reconstruction expert explained that he reviewed police reports and photographs, carefully studied an enhanced version of the PI's videotape and closely examined about 1,400 laser-aided measurements taken of the parking lot at the Nassau Bay Hilton to help him arrive at his conclusions.

Verbally re-creating the route taken by the Mercedes and the fatal impact for the jury, Irwin said the defendant's vehicle was traveling about 15 to 20 mph when it clipped the rear of Gail's SUV. Then it sideswiped the parked car and slammed into the victim, who was standing by the open door, and carried him for a short distance on the hood. David's body was likely hurled from the hood when the Mercedes bumped over a curb surrounding the grassy median, the witness testified. The body landed 64 feet from the point of impact, he said. That was considerably further than estimates of some of the eyewitnesses.

"Human bodies do not bounce," Irwin declared. "You cannot give it speed the car does not have. It needs something else. It needs more than one push."

The expert explained that his reconstruction

indicated that after sideswiping the Navigator and hitting David, the Mercedes returned and circled him as many as three times. But it never crossed over the center of the loop, where the bloodstains indicated the body of the mortally injured man was lying.

Irwin seemed to be a good witness with excellent credentials and his testimony sounded impressive. Expert witnesses know their jobs and they usually, although not always, turn in a good performance on the stand. That's especially true during direct examination when they are being questioned by friendly attorneys for either the defense or the prosecution. But Irwin was a defense witness and when it was Magness' turn to ask the questions, her cross-examination was far from cordial.

Everyone was already fresh from the evidentiary hearing the previous day, so the prosecutor had a good idea what the witness was going to say. She was well-prepared to make him back up his testimony with solid facts. Magness was intent on poking holes in his conclusions, disassembling his testimony and challenging everything the $195-an-hour expert witness had to say.

Under her aggressive questioning, Irwin conceded that the victim's 5-foot-9-inch body could have extended well beyond the blood spot. That was the opening the prosecutor was shooting for. "What you're really telling this jury is ... you can't tell them she never ran over that body again because you don't know where the body was," Magness bore in, making the statement a question. Irwin was boxed in with no place to escape.

"Fair enough," he said.

The brashly confident prosecutor attacked his presentation as "a whole lot of math" and suggested his entire theory could be wrong if even a single element — such as the presumed location of the PI who shot the video — was wrong.

After the witness agreed with her that more information was better than less information when reconstructing an accident, he also conceded that eyewitness accounts might be worth taking into consideration. It was also true, he agreed under the withering hail of questions, that he hadn't interviewed any of the state's witnesses who said David was run over more than once.

Magness then demanded to know if three eyewitnesses who said the victim was run over multiple times would change his mind about his conclusions. Irwin said it wouldn't.

"Four eyewitnesses?" she asked. "Ten eyewitnesses?"

Irwin stuck to his guns. "No ma'am," he replied.

The tough-minded prosecutor responded with another question posed as a statement. "You're pretty much wedded to your opinion regardless of how many eyewitnesses say otherwise?"

"Yes," the witness said. Then he fudged his response a bit. "It's not like I wrote the Bible. I'm only human and I can be wrong," he confessed. "But I do not believe I'm wrong."

The prosecutor was just getting up a good head of steam and she kept the witness on the hot seat. After Irwin said he relied heavily on the videotape shot at the crime scene, Magness moved in for another hail of questions aimed at showing a possible gap in the filming that failed to capture images of the car running over the body more than once.

"Somebody had to get the camera ready, to push the button," she declared. "That could take four or five seconds. They'd have to reach for the camera and get it into position. That could take another five or six seconds."

"That sounds like conjecture to me — but it's not impossible," the witness replied.

"And what if in those 10 seconds, what if the car isn't going in circles? What if it's backing over the body? Is that a possibility?" Magness demanded.

"Yes," Irwin said.

The hard-driving, dynamic prosecutor had made a strong point for the state before court was adjourned Friday afternoon, marking the end of an exhausting day and an exhausting week for everyone involved, especially for the defendant. Clara's face was drawn and tight when she left the courtroom accompanied by her legal team and her faithful in-laws for the weekend break.

Judge Davies had warned her and her attorneys three times that she could be kicked out of her own trial if she didn't show better control of her emotions. Clara had two full days to spend with her twins, friends and family while steeling herself for what could be the final week of a trial that would determine where and how she spent the rest of her life. She was aware that it could also be the last weekend she would spend with her boys for years.

When testimony resumed Monday morning the sensational courtroom proceeding had been eclipsed by a greater, national tragedy that occurred in the skies 40 miles above Texas on Saturday, Feb. 1.

The breakup of the Space Shuttle Columbia during re-entry after a two-week journey shocked the world and thrust Americans all over the country into mourning for seven

courageous astronauts who died when they
were only a few minutes away from a landing.
Grief was especially intense among families of
the astronauts and among colleagues who
monitored the flight from the Johnson Space
Center in Houston's southern suburbs where so
many major figures in the courtroom drama
taking place at the Harris County Criminal
Justice Center lived and worked.

Before the trial was reconvened, Judge Davies
asked everyone in the courtroom to stand and
recite the Pledge of Allegiance in honor of the
dead astronauts. Then everyone got back to the
grim business of the murder case.

Testimony reopened with appearances by
Space Center Orthodontics employees, who
retraced the flirtation between their boss and
the sexy new receptionist that developed into
the disastrous romantic affair.

"You could almost feel the chemistry between
them," Diana Sherrill recalled of her late
employer and the receptionist. "He wasn't in
love. He was just infatuated."

Sherrill testified that she was so concerned
that she talked about her suspicions with Clara.
"I told her she needed to protect her marriage,
not to ignore anything out of the ordinary,
maybe go to counseling to get help. Sometimes

men go through a change in life and maybe that's what was happening to David."

Clara "was frightened a little" by the revelation, she said.

Magness conducted the cross-examination and went right to work attempting to soften the image of the victim as a marital cheat with a strong streak of meanness. "With the exception of this affair, David was a good guy, wasn't he?" the prosecutor asked

"Yes," the witness responded.

Office Manager Cathy Davis said Clara was head-over-heels in love with her husband. "He was the love of her life and it was very obvious," she testified.

Magness suggested that some of the testimony from office employees may have been linked to a personal dislike of the receptionist. She continued through a series of queries to raise the possibility that the new woman in the office may have threatened the job security of other members of the staff by taking over their responsibilities and becoming the boss's pet.

"She didn't help me much," Davis said.

The witness barely got the remark out of her mouth, before Magness let loose with a rapid-fire barrage of new queries about how the defendant dealt with anger.

"My question is: You've never seen her angry?" Magness asked.

"No," Davis responded.

"You don't know what she's capable of doing when angry?"

"No," the witness again replied.

"You've never seen that side of the defendant?" Magness continued.

"No."

The exchange clearly produced the result the prosecutor was working for. Some jurors glanced away from the witness and peered at the defendant as if they were wondering: What was the patrician-looking woman sitting at the defense table really capable of doing when her anger boiled over?

Testimony by John Tyler, the Baylor College of Medicine public affairs specialist and Bible student, reinforced the image of a woman who had been driven to the edge until her emotions boiled over into a firestorm of anger and deadly violence. Tyler described his shock when David grabbed his wife by the face and hurled her to the floor. The witness used his hands to demonstrate how the orthodontist pulled his wife off his mistress.

"It scared me to death," Tyler said. "Up until that time, the fight had been just two women, not to minimize that. But when he put his hands on her, it brought it to a whole new level. It certainly looked violent to me."

Magness pounced on the statement in cross-examination, reminding the witness: "You told police that the defendant was punching Bridges, ripping her clothing and wouldn't let go!" Others had already tried to separate the women without any success, the prosecutor prompted. She asked if David's action when he finally intervened was unreasonable.

"He used more force than I would have," the soft-spoken PR man responded.

"Was the defendant mad?" Magness asked.

"Furious," the witness replied.

Tuesday morning, the woman who just about everyone in the courtroom had been waiting to hear and see was called to the stand as a potentially hostile witness for the defense — Gail Bridges.

Most members of the local legal community who were closely following the trial agreed that calling the defendant's rival to the stand was excellent strategy by the defense. Famous criminal defense attorney Percy Foreman once declared that a good defense should include testimony from a witness that jurors could hate more than the defendant. As the "other woman" in the tragedy, Gail seemed to fit perfectly into the Foreman mold of perfect witness.

Looking tiny, frail and vulnerable in a tailored black pantsuit and gray turtleneck sweater, the 39-year-old divorcée who helped ruin the defendant's marriage and played a starring role in the nightmare that cost David his life was sworn in. At the request of Gail's attorneys, the judge barred photographers from taking pictures of her. Judge Davies also ordered the defense not to delve too deeply into explicit details of the hanky-panky that occurred between the star-crossed lovers.

Although she was tearful and trembling at times, Gail cooperated so fully under questioning that the judge never officially designated her as a hostile witness — a move that would have allowed the defense more latitude in questioning.

Defense co-counsel Emily Munoz asked the questions and she barely started her direct examination before Magness unleashed the first of what quickly became a barrage of objections. Judge Davies eventually delivered a sharp warning to the defense counsel to stick to questions "relevant to this case" and to steer clear of going too deeply into the relationship between the lovers.

From the first moment her rival was called to the witness stand, Clara studiously avoided looking at her. She stared icily to the side throughout the testimony. The witness was clearly nervous and looked dwarfed by her chair next to the bench as she hunched her shoulders protectively and replied to questions in a soft, little-girl voice.

Gail shocked some in the courtroom and drew a bitter frown from the defendant, still staring to the side, when she said she thought it was OK to have a sexual relationship with her boss because he told her that he and his wife had an "open marriage." David said his wife had been involved in an extramarital affair so he was also free to date other women, the witness declared.

"I had the impression she knew the whole time."

Under Munoz's skillful prompting, Gail retraced her rapid salary increase and hefty bonuses at Space Center Orthodontics and said she was unaware that she was the only front-office employee being treated so generously.

She was having lunch with her boss on April 5 when he first suggested they date, she said. The following month they had sex with each other for the first time when they checked into the hotel at the Galleria.

Asked if her relationship with her boss created turmoil at the clinic, the witness said she didn't know if those were "the right words."

"It's safe to say the relationship started affecting

patients, isn't it?" Munoz queried. "Didn't patients
begin to ask if you and David were married?"

"I cannot say that," the witness answered.
"But you leaned over and put your butt in his
face?" Munoz was referring to an alleged incident Lindsey mentioned in her testimony.

"I do not remember that," Gail crisply replied.

The defense attorney moved on to the nasty
scene when Clara stormed into Space Center
Orthodontics and fired Gail. The witness said
she was surprised and confused by the behavior.

"It was never really clear," she explained. "Clara
told me I was fired and David told me I was not."
Gail said she didn't realize that she had really
lost her job until he died.

The witness drew a small gasp of stunned
surprise from a few spectators when she acknowledged filing a federal complaint against Clara to
recover severance, overtime and vacation pay.

Gail testified that she didn't know David
promised his wife he would break off his affair
with her during their last dinner date. When
they finished their drinks at the hotel and
rented a room, she said she thought they "had
a future together."

After Gail described the catfight in the lobby,
Munoz asked if she blamed Clara for being angry.

"No, ma'am," the witness replied. "I do not."

Wednesday morning, Clara was called to the witness stand, ending speculation about whether she would appear in her own defense. Reportedly going against the advice of her lawyers, she had decided to testify. Other members of the local legal community who were closely monitoring the trial were divided in their opinions about whether Clara's testimony would help or harm her case.

The manner in which she handled herself on the witness stand and how she came across to the jury were expected to determine if she made the right choice. Would Clara come off sympathetically as a spurned wife who suddenly snapped or as a bloodthirsty murderess who deliberately mowed down her philandering husband with her luxury sedan and then continued to roll over his body in a series of macabre victory laps?

Dressed as usual in a crisply pressed business suit and with her hair returned to its natural brunette, swept back and held with a tiny bow, she looked self-assured and confident, ready for the ordeal ahead. She even permitted herself a cautious smile as she slid into the witness chair alongside the bench.

Under Parnham's gentle questioning, Clara described herself and her husband as best friends. "We were very much in love. We were mature —

both of us had gone through a divorce and knew exactly who we were," she testified. "No couple was better suited than us to be a perfect team."

Clara traced their business partnership and firmly denied that she was involved in an affair of her own or that she and her husband agreed to an "open marriage," which would leave both of them free to pursue romance with others.

When questioning moved on to David's affair and her first confrontation with his mistress, Clara turned to sarcasm. She replied in high-pitched tones designed to mimic Gail's voice while describing the scene at Space Center Orthodontics when she fired Gail. Clara said the receptionist turned to David and whimpered, "What should I do? Maybe if I left for a couple of hours and came back, she will have calmed down?"

The impersonation brought smiles and giggles from spectators and several members of the jury. Some jurors appeared to be charmed by the sympathetic witness. But the performance brought a disapproving frown from the judge.

Parnham's efforts to create a smoothly fluid account of events were frustrated by a string of objections from Magness. The objections led Judge Davies to repeatedly remind the witness to stay on course.

During the lunch break, the defendant's 62-year-old lead attorney collapsed in a hallway. Court was adjourned for the remainder of the day and the next day after the ailing attorney was rushed by ambulance to St. Luke's Episcopal Hospital. At a hastily organized news conference, Odom blamed his law partner's collapse on exhaustion and a touch of the flu. The combination of stress and illness "made him lightheaded and he had a fainting spell," the lawyer explained.

Although he looked a bit peaked, when court resumed Parnham was back in harness and primed to continue the direct examination as Clara was recalled to the witness stand.

The witness drew gasps of shock and outrage from several female spectators when she retraced the demeaning experience at the sports bar the night she scribbled down her husband's comparisons of wife and mistress on napkins.

David told her that his lover was "petite with the perfect fit to sleep with, holding her all night," she told the jury.

Parnham asked how she felt about that.

"I couldn't believe he could sleep holding her all night because we had never slept like that," Clara replied.

The napkins, with their telltale notations,

were introduced as evidence. Earlier, some of
the same spectators nodded their heads in
seemingly silent agreement as she described
her humiliation when she first learned of her
husband's philandering and realized that she
was the last to know.

In an obvious move to refute Gail's testimony
about the reputed "open marriage" between his
client and her husband, Parnham asked if
David ever suggested they have sex with other
people. Prosecutors objected. Judge Davies
sustained the objection before the witness
could answer.

The emotional strain showed, but Clara managed to hang tenuously onto her composure
until questioning turned to the violent confrontations at the hotel. She was in tears again
when she admitted vandalizing Gail's car and
bending the back windshield wiper. "It was so
painful in my hand," she sobbed, "but it was
more painful in my heart."

As she testified about her emotional and
mental state after she and her stepdaughter
climbed into the Mercedes following the brawl
in the lobby, her remarks became slightly dis-
connected. "I was in so much pain, it was a
physical pain that I was feeling. I wasn't feeling
anything." The witness's testimony became

erratic, with stops and starts as she took deep breaths and her eyes welled with tears.

"Suddenly I thought about smashing my car against her car and then I (picked) up speed."

Clara said she wanted to smash her rival's SUV but "I think I closed my eyes. After that, I didn't know who was driving. Everything seemed like a dream. That was a crazy moment. I had never been through a blackout like that before."

She remembered her stepdaughter screaming for her to stop, but even then she didn't realize she had struck and run over her husband, Clara said.

After David was struck down, she said she got out of the car and peered down at his mangled body lying in the parking lot. "I couldn't understand what he was doing there," she testified. "I had just seen him running and I didn't know how he got there. I said, 'David, David, please talk to me.' "

Judge Davies called a temporary halt three times during the testimony to confer with attorneys while the defendant struggled to compose herself. The judge was clearly impatient and determined to cut through the emotional disruption and get the testimony and trial back on track. Unlike her behavior on the stand the previous day, Clara was having a hard time handling the gloomy exchanges and she repeatedly broke down into agonized fits of sobbing. At other times she covered her face with her folded hands. The testimony was heartrending and spectators wiped at moist eyes and tear-streaked cheeks while the witness continued her torturous recital.

When Magness moved in for cross-examination, Clara refused to admit that she was in a rage after catching her husband at the hotel with her rival. "I was extremely upset," she said of her reaction when she saw the lovers step out of the elevator. "He was holding Gail's hand the way he used to hold my hand when I was special to him."

"You weren't angry?" Magness asked, her face and tone mirroring her obvious disbelief.

"No, not yet," the witness replied.

Pecking away at Clara's statement that she was intent only on striking the Navigator and didn't know her husband was standing next to it, Magness eventually got her to concede that she saw David running to the left while the Mercedes was bearing down on him.

"All this happened in a fraction of a second," Clara said. "I didn't have time to think."

Magness also used Clara's statement to police early the morning after her husband died in an effort to show that she intentionally ran over her husband.

"My question is: Did you not tell police that you wanted to separate him from her?" the prosecutor demanded.

"That statement makes no sense. That was a transcript of a tape that was very difficult to understand," Clara responded.

"I'm asking you, Mrs. Harris, when you came around the Navigator," Magness bored in, "did you see him?"

"I saw three people standing next to the Navigator, I didn't know who they were."

"You saw the look on his face and just wanted to get him apart from her," the prosecutor continued, her voice indicating that such a statement was difficult to believe.

"You've got it all wrong," Clara replied.

On Monday, Feb. 10, the trial was in its third week and rapidly winding down when Gerald and Mildred Harris and David's brother, Gerald Jr., testified as character witnesses for the defendant. They described Clara as a truthful, law-abiding individual. "I love her very much," Mildred Harris told the jury, while smiling at the defendant. "She's really more like a daughter than a daughter-in-law."

After her son confessed his affair with the

receptionist, Clara was "very nervous, very concerned about David," the witness continued. "She didn't know what to do."

During her cross-examination of the 69-year-old white-haired grandmother, Magness pointed out that their son's widow could have kept the twins from seeing them if they chose not to support her.

Mildred Harris' smile vanished. "I don't know what you are trying to get me to say," she replied. "But there is no problem with me getting to see those children."

Gerald Harris Sr. said of the defendant: "When she married David she became our daughter. We love her and we are trying to do the best we can for her." Despite his distress over David's philandering, the elder Harris made it clear he also treasured comforting memories of his son. "He was a good Christian man and he loved his family," the witness recalled.

David's father also addressed the family's attitude toward the woman who used her luxury car to run down and kill their son and brother — a position that so many outsiders found almost impossible to comprehend.

"What most people don't understand is that if you're a child of God, you are forgiven of all your sins and if you don't forgive others, it's hard to say you're forgiven," the deeply religious witness explained. "We are empowered by God's love to forgive everyone, everything. We're just little people that love our family. We have a great God and he's big enough to make our hearts big enough to forgive everything."

After the poignant testimony of the Harris family members concluded, co-counsel McWilliams attempted to persuade the judge outside the presence of the jury to permit questioning about the reputed lesbian relationship between Gail and her chum, Julie Knight.

Davies blocked a previous effort to pursue the line of questioning by the defense team, which contended the women were trying to shake David down for cash. And she rejected the proposal again.

With the possibility of delving into the personal relationship between Gail and her friend settled once and for all, the defense rested and stepped aside for the prosecution to begin presenting rebuttal witnesses. Closing arguments were not expected to start until Wednesday, but Judge Davies had been around too long to take chances.

She instructed the jury to bring toothbrushes and other necessities to court on Tuesday, just in case they were sent off to begin deliberations earlier than expected and had to stay away from their homes overnight because they were sequestered. With that said, the jury was ready to begin hearing the rebuttal witnesses.

Rolando Saenz, a Houston Police Department investigator, testified that defense collision reconstructionist Steve Irwin's conclusion that David was run over only one time was flawed.

Saenz said his own inspection of the evidence, including the turning radius of the Mercedes-Benz and bloodstains, showed that the victim could indeed have been struck repeatedly. The witness had investigated more than 10,000 collisions involving vehicles over nearly two decades.

Saenz said it was possible to change the turning radius of a car if while making a left hand turn a driver caused it to skid to the right. By using a skid to make a much tighter circle, the defendant could have struck the victim more than once. Saenz also noted that separate, distinct blood stains and a rub mark he observed on the undercarriage of the Mercedes indicated David was run over at least twice. The witness said he had concluded that the defendant probably made a wider arc around the Lincoln Navigator than Irwin suggested. And that could have provided Clara a clear look at her husband standing near the open driver's door of the SUV.

During cross-examination, Saenz conceded he only viewed the undercarriage of the Mercedes in photographs and didn't interview witnesses on his own.

Linda Haley, a fingerprint expert with the Harris County Sheriff's Department, also testified that fingerprints found on the hood of the Mercedes belonged to the victim. Under cross-examination, she conceded that she couldn't tell the jury how they got there.

Ashok Moza, one of the tennis players attracted by the commotion at the hotel, was also called as a rebuttal witness by the prosecution and said he saw the Mercedes run over an object twice. When he investigated, he discovered that what he had thought was a duffel bag was a human being.

Early Wednesday morning Magness began closing arguments by stating the obvious.

"David Harris' affair was immoral and wrong," but the solution for his wife was to get divorced, the prosecutor declared. "She should do like every other woman in Harris County and take him to the cleaners ... Get his house, car, kids — make him wish he was dead. But you don't get to kill him."

Magness said the defense had developed three strategies to defend their client: It was an accident, vilify and beat up on the victim, and a "just lost it" scenario. She pointed out that Texas law doesn't provide for an accident defense and observed that the theory had already been picked apart. "When you run over a person again and again and again," she said, "your intent is to hurt him, your intent is to kill him."

The gritty prosecutor also pointed out that the cheating husband was the subject of hours of negative testimony critical of his behavior. Magness indicated she favored the third scenario, but with a twist not exploited by the defense. "Just lost it — that's what murder is. It's the momentary loss of respect for human life and taking it. Did she lose it? You bet!"

Continuing to build on that theme, Magness declared, "The bottom line is this: She got mad, engaged in reckless, knowing conduct and David is dead because of it. Though you've heard her called a good mother, a loving spouse, a good dentist, at this point it's time to call her what she is," the prosecutor said of Clara. "And that's a murderer!"

Parnham, when the defense had their turn in closing arguments, concentrated on reminding the jury of the defendant's love for her husband and of the defense contention that David's grisly death wasn't planned. Even though Clara endured "deceptions after deceptions," the lawyer argued, his client never meant to kill her husband. "Had she intended to kill David, her husband, would she ever have taken her stepdaughter with her?" he asked. "It never would have been imagined."

The lawyer also argued that Clara wouldn't have been able to see her husband standing beside the Lincoln Navigator in the hotel parking lot in time to stop. Alluding to the grainy video shot by the Blue Moon investigator, he contended that as Clara circled David while he was lying on the pavement, the circles grew tighter and tighter.

"After the third circle, she parks right next to the body," he said. "She kneels next to David and begs him to stay with her. And you know, the turns missed him."

Moving on to the couple's life before the affair, then to "the other woman," Parnham told the jury that the couple had a beautiful marriage. "A marriage made in heaven until someone knocks on the door of the home and someone knocks on the heart of the family. Gail Thompson Bridges is a homewrecker," the defense attorney thundered. "I don't care how you slice it, she was after David, after his heart. And she interceded, knowing this woman was married to that man and she enticed and seduced him into a relationship.

"I'm not up here to vilify David Harris. This woman still loves him," Parnham declared, nodding toward the defendant. "I'm not here to vilify David Harris in the mind of Lindsey. He's her father. But he made bad choices, folks, bad decisions."

It was almost noon when closing statements were completed. Judge Davies read her instructions to the jury and the panel of nine women and three men filed out of the courtroom to begin deliberations.

CHAPTER 12

The verdict

The jury of nine women and three men was faced with several choices. They could acquit the defendant of all charges, which seemed to be highly improbable. It appeared more likely the panel would return a verdict of guilty to one of three possible offenses carrying a wide rage of sentences. The charges and penalties included:

MURDER — A first-degree felony, conviction of the offense carried a penalty ranging from five to 99 years or life in prison and up to a $10,000 fine. A life sentence would provide eligibility for parole after 30 years.

During the sentencing phase of the trial, the jury could also consider "sudden passion" and reduce the punishment to two to 20 years behind bars with a fine of up to $10,000. If the jury found "sudden passion" to be a mitigating factor and settled on a prison sentence of 10 years or less, Clara could actually be given a slap on the wrist with immediate release on five years probation. A sentence of more than 10 years, even accompanied by a finding of sudden passion, would mean that she had to serve half of her prison term before becoming eligible for parole.

MANSLAUGHTER — A second-degree felony, conviction provided for a sentence of from two to 20 years in prison and a fine of up to $10,000.

CRIMINALLY NEGLIGENT HOMICIDE — According to the Texas penal code, the offense is a state jail felony. Conviction provides for confinement in a state jail for not more than two years or less than 180 days and a fine of up to $10,000. If the jury determined a deadly weapon was used in commission of the crime, the charges would become a third-degree felony, punishable by two to 10 years in prison and a fine of up to $10,000.

The most important distinction between the possible findings was the degree or absence of intent and jurors deliberated seven hours Wednesday before calling it quits for the day and being transported to a hotel where they were sequestered. Early Thursday morning the panel briefly continued deliberations before notifying the judge at about 9 a.m. that a verdict was reached.

Flanked by Parnham and Munoz, who held tightly to her hands, the somber defendant stood dry-eyed while the jury was polled and one by one reported a unanimous verdict finding her guilty of the most serious of the possible offenses — murder. Two members of the jury sobbed as they reported their finding. Clara appeared to have been prepared for the bad news and sat quietly and outwardly composed at the defense table.

The panel also found that Clara used the Mercedes-Benz as a deadly weapon. According to Texas criminal codes, the deadly weapon finding meant that she had to serve at least half of her sentence before becoming eligible for parole. If she was sent to prison, she would also have to remain behind bars while the case was on appeal.

But the penalty was still to be determined during the sentencing phase of the trial, which would include more emotionally draining testimony from the most innocent victim of the tragedy that tore the David Harris family apart. According to Texas law, the jury, not the judge, would decide the punishment.

Lindsey sat behind the prosecutor's table to listen to the verdict. Her paternal grandparents, still loyal to their daughter-in-law, sat on the defense side.

As the penalty phase began, the girl returned to the stand and traced the terrible emotional toll that witnessing her father's horrible death had taken on her. The pretty teenager said that after returning to Columbus her grades at school plummeted and she dropped out of her favorite activities.

"I slit my wrists," she confided.

"Was that on more than one occasion?" the prosecutor asked.

"Yes," Lindsey replied.

Once more Clara had heard more than she could handle and she began loudly sobbing, causing prosecutors to ask that the jury be removed from the courtroom. The judge complied and ordered a short break to give Clara an opportunity to get her emotions under control.

"I'm sorry, Lindsey! I'm sorry, baby!" Clara wailed from the defense table as the jury began filing out.

"Be quiet!" Davies commanded from the bench.

Clara continued to cry out, "I'm sorry. I'm sorry."

For the fourth time during the agonizing near three-week proceeding, Davies sharply reprimanded Clara and warned that she would be removed from the courtroom if she continued to disrupt the proceedings.

"Don't blow it!" the judge advised.

When the determined jurist issued a similar warning to spectators who were having trouble with their emotions, two women got up from their seats and filed out of the courtroom.

Resuming her heartbreaking testimony, Lindsey told the jury that she had a great relationship with her father and when she was in Ohio she talked to him on the telephone every day. "We were the same person," the teenager said. "We finished each other's sentences." She and her father also shared mutual interests including music, athletics and dentistry.

"I planned to come to college down here and

spend the rest of my life down here," she said. "Everything was planned. It was perfect. And then it was ruined!"

The testimony turned agonizingly grim again as Lindsey recalled the harrowing minutes in the Mercedes when she realized her father's life was ending in front of her eyes. "It was terrifying. She was killing him. I would never see him again. I never got to say goodbye. I only got to spend 16½ years with him. I had plans. It just wasn't fair," the teenager said of her loss.

Returning again to the dreadful emotional toll the experience took on her, Lindsey said she went into depression, underwent counseling and was prescribed mood-altering drugs. "It made things worse," she said of the medication. "I was just numb!"

The teenager told the jury she was estranged from her grandparents because of their support for her stepmother. She suggested they may have been motivated in part by financial considerations involving her father's estate.

Gerald Harris Sr. was the first witness called by the defense in the punishment phase and firmly denied his granddaughter's claim that financial considerations had anything to do with the family's support of Clara. "No, sir," he told the jury. "That hasn't anything to do with it. I don't expect to get anything out of it. Our motivation stems from the word 'forgiveness.' "

Echoing his previous testimony, the witness added: "This tragedy has been a strong blow to our family. God has forgiven our sins. We can forgive a member of our family when she has erred."

Harris, his wife, and son, Gerald Jr. were among seven witnesses who testified during the sentencing phase that Clara was a good candidate for probation. The family minister, neighbors and the former Colombian consul-general for Texas and Oklahoma were among others who testified in support of probation.

The defense team presented strong testimony to show that Clara could meet the conditions of probation, including holding down a job, supporting her boys, living as a law-abiding citizen and meeting community service requirements. But loss of her dental license because of the murder conviction would prevent her from continuing to earn income or perform community service by working in her profession.

When the hearing concluded for the day, Clara wasn't accompanied out of the courtroom by her attorneys and loyal Harris family members as she was throughout the earlier proceedings. With the jury's verdict, she had become a convicted murderess, her bail was no longer in force and she was no longer free to return home to her twins.

After being allowed to say goodbye to her in-laws and other well-wishers, she was instructed to remove her simple gold wedding band, wristwatch and other jewelry. Then she was escorted from the courtroom by law enforcement officers and driven to the Harris County Jail on nearby Baker Street to spend the night. At the jail she was issued an orange jumpsuit, then locked in a 300-square-foot, four-woman cell with one other inmate. A camera in the cell, mounted on the ceiling, was monitored by guards to keep a 24-hour watch on the two women.

Friday morning, attorneys once more delivered summations, this time tilting swords over the proposed penalty to be ordered for a woman convicted of murdering her husband.

"Probation is not appropriate in this case. If the situation were reversed and David Harris had run her down, would you consider probation?" the prosecutor asked the jury. Then she commiserated with the panelists over the difficult decision they had to make. "Doing the right thing doesn't always feel good, does it?" she observed. "That's the position you're in right now, because the right thing in this case is not going to be easy. But I know that you'll do it. I know that it will be hard, but I'm respectfully requesting that you send her to prison, because she has earned it and because David Harris deserves it."

Parnham pleaded with the jury to bypass jail time and decide on no more than 10 years of probation for his client. Sudden passion drove her to commit the act that cost her husband's life when she discovered him and his mistress leaving the same hotel where they were married, he declared.

"Clara was respected and loved by neighbors, colleagues and employees," he said. "She worked hard, she is and was a good mother and a good wife. She had respect and she will be able to abide by the terms and conditions of probation."

Clara was dressed once more in civilian clothes, but showed the effects of a night in jail while she listened to the final arguments. She appeared haggard and drained, her carefully tailored clothes looked suddenly too big for her and for the first time in the month-long trial, she wore no makeup or jewelry.

The tears came, as they had before, when her lawyer retraced her attributes and talked of the love and faith expressed by her family and friends. "She is loved by the family that was closest to David," the lead defense attorney declared. "We know Gerald and Mildred and

Gerry don't want those boys ripped away from the last parent they have on Earth ... Putting Clara in the penitentiary is not going to do anything to make things right."

When Magness went back on the offense, the convicted woman buried her head in her hands and nodded in disagreement. The prosecutor urged the jury to discount the defense's repeated accounts of Clara's suffering at the hands of her unfaithful and insensitive husband.

"Suffering is lying on the asphalt like some kind of wounded animal, drowning in your own blood while your teenage daughter watched," she declared.

The prosecutor suggested that Clara was using her little boys as "a shield" to win probation. She reminded the jury that the boys would be well cared for, regardless of what happened to their mother. "It's not fair to ask you to care about those boys more than she did on the night she killed their father," Magness said. "She ought to take credit for making herself a single parent."

The assistant DA reminded the jury that Clara never claimed to be acting under the influence of sudden passion when she repeatedly ran over her husband's body with the heavy Mercedes. "She never said to you that she was mad. She never admitted she was angry, there was fear, terror or resentment," the prosecutor declared. "The most she said to you was 'I was upset.'"

Magness dwelled at length on the emotional trauma suffered by the dead man's daughter. She blamed Clara for depriving the teenager of having her father witness her high school graduation and of walking down the aisle with him at her wedding. "Her life is forever changed and she didn't even get to say goodbye."

Several spectators were in tears, audibly sobbing as the prosecutor retraced the horror Lindsey experienced while riding in the car as it repeatedly ran over her father. "Lindsey told you of cutting her own flesh because she was so overwhelmed by the pain she experienced," Magness reminded the jury. "That's something you should consider."

The trial was taking a toll on everyone involved, including members of the jury and court officers. Even the determined and usually unflappable prosecutor betrayed a chink in her hard-boiled exterior. Tears welled in her eyes and her voice quivered during her hard-hitting summation. Court reporter Tamra Parks also was noticed having trouble hiding her emotions.

After the summations and before the verdict, defense co-counsel Emily Munoz used the emotional displays as the basis for a motion to declare a mistrial. She said the prosecutor was "teary-eyed" and the court reporter reached for a tissue and wiped at her eyes — all in view of the jury. The court reporter's actions were "prejudicial," Munoz argued. The defense attorney explained that she didn't protest earlier because she didn't want to interrupt her courtroom rival's "powerful summation."

The crusty, implacable judge rejected the motion and pointed out that there were a lot of tears in the courtroom at that time. "It is a little late for me to do anything now," she observed.

The panel deliberated six hours before returning to the courtroom on the afternoon of Friday, Feb. 14, to report that a decision was reached on Clara's punishment. The jury agreed that Clara acted with "sudden passion," but ordered the maximum penalty under the law.

As Judge Davies read the verdict, the defendant threw her head back in anguish. Wailing in torment, she dropped limply into her chair. Parnham did what he could to console her by rubbing her heaving shoulders while she buried her face in Munoz's lap. The co-counsel protectively cradled the sobbing woman's head in her arms.

Neither side won a total victory. Clara wouldn't

escape with mere probation, nor would she be sentenced to serve 99 years.

Clara was handcuffed and stood between her lawyers in front of the bench for formal sentencing. She had no response when asked if she had anything to say and moments later Judge Davies sentenced her to custody of the Institutional Division of the Texas Department of Criminal Justice for the maximum sentence of 20 years. In accordance with the criminal codes, she had to serve half of that before becoming eligible for parole. She was also assessed the maximum possible fine, $10,000.

At best, Clara would be 55 years old and her twins would be 14 before she could expect to be a free woman again. That, of course, was dependent on a parole board agreeing to her release as soon as she was eligible and Texas doesn't have a reputation for taking it easy on convicted murderers. So early parole was far from a sure thing, even if Clara behaved as expected and was a cooperative, well-behaved inmate.

A few minutes after the sentence was passed, Clara was led out of Judge Davies' courtroom by Harris County Sheriff's deputies for the final time. She was driven back to the jail and held there for transfer to the Texas State Corrections

Department for determination of a permanent prison assignment.

In a touch of unintended but grotesquely poetic irony, Clara was sent to prison on Valentine's Day — on what would have been the 11th anniversary of her marriage to David. At her request, without publicity or fanfare, a neighbor drove to the cemetery in Pearland later that day and left a large floral bouquet on David's grave.

For the time being, Clara's boys would be staying with their paternal grandparents. Parnham later told the hostess of CNN's *Connie Chung Tonight* that the grandparents had already initiated a legal proceeding, supported by Clara, to assume custody of the boys while their mother was in prison.

The toddlers had been told their father was in Heaven. Now someone would have to explain where their mom was.

With the case and sentencing decided, just about all the court officers except the judge had a few words for the press. A dismal drizzle of rain added a touch of gloom to the already somber atmosphere outside the courthouse as reporters gathered around the front steps for a summing up of the events that occurred inside during the past three weeks.

"After hearing all the evidence, this jury

recognized the case for what it was and that is the senseless taking of a human life," Magness observed. "Their verdict recognized Mrs. Harris' conduct and they didn't excuse it. They felt all of the things, I think, that she felt and they factored that into their decision. But I still think they sent a message that was pretty clear.

"And it's simply this: If you unlawfully take a human life, for whatever reason, you're going to jail. And that's the way it is in our county and that's the way it ought to be." The prosecutor admitted that she was personally overwhelmed by just how tragic the whole affair was, but said it seemed to her "that the victim was getting lost in the process."

Standing with his wife and stepdaughter, James Shank said they were pleased with the verdict and the fact that justice was served. "This has been a very difficult time, a very trying time for all of us, especially Lindsey," he said. "We are relieved that the trial is finally over and now it's time for us to go home and begin the healing process."

Minutes earlier inside the courtroom, Lindsey burst into tears when Maria Gonzalez, the boys' nanny, walked across the courtroom to where the girl was sitting with her mother and stepfather on the prosecutors' side and hugged her.

Hector Gonzalez, Clara's cousin from Colombia and apparently no relation to Maria, ardently supported Clara throughout the ordeal, and stated the obvious: "She's broken up!" Then he made it clear he wasn't giving up on his cousin. "But we will see this to the end," he said, "and we hope to see a better light for Clara."

In later statements, juror Dan Walker remarked, "In our society, you cannot not punish her for killing her husband in the fashion she did." Walker added that he was convinced of the defendant's guilt and voted for the 20 year sentence because he believed that Houston accident investigator Rolando Saenz's testimony was more credible than that of the defense expert.

Parnham was flanked by his somber colleagues, Munoz and McWilliams, when he vowed to appeal the verdict. He said there were many grounds and issues in the appellate process, but appeals might focus on expert testimony and evidence such as the two-hour-long audiotape of his client's statement to police in the early hours immediately following her husband's death that wasn't admitted as evidence. The tape, the defense lawyer argued, would reveal Clara's turbulent state of mind during the interrogation and that portions were quoted out of context at the trial.

CONCLUSION

It would be difficult to conceive of a more heartrending murder case than the unhappy saga of David and Clara Harris, and the many other men, women and children whose lives were forever blighted by the terrible occurrences of July 24, 2002, and the events leading up to the tragedy.

A fairy-tale marriage blessed with a healthy set of twins was shattered, leaving the husband dead, the wife facing long, lonely years in prison and two little boys without their father and their mother. The exciting and promising life of a teenager eagerly looking forward to all the challenges and rewards of responsible adulthood was turned into a nightmare and sent into a tailspin. Gail Bridges, already reeling from cruel accusations that she was a lesbian, became nationally notorious as an adulteress, homewrecker and sexy seductress whose selfishness and poor choices were at the heart of the tragedy and helped lead to the death of the man she claimed to love.

In Colombia, Clara's mother was left to grieve over the catastrophe that overtook her brilliant, ambitious, level-headed and loving only child and the seemingly perfect mate she was married to. Other relatives, friends, neighbors and employees in the chain of dental offices were heartsick over the disaster that shattered the marriage and the lives of David and Clara. And two proud grandparents, suddenly left without a son and the woman they looked upon as a daughter, were also left estranged from one beloved grandchild and faced their so-called golden years with the responsibility of caring for two children who were still in preschool.

A week after Clara's conviction, the elder Harrises were granted joint custody of the twins after a nonjury trial in Brazoria County. The decision was almost immediately challenged by Houston lawyer Pamela Hoerster, who was appointed by a Galveston County judge to represent the twins in their father's probate case and complained that she wasn't notified about the hearing in Brazoria County.

Hoerster filed a brief, asking family court Judge K. Randall Hustetler for a new trial, a change of venue to Galveston County and an order sanctioning the twins' mother and grandparents for filing the action in Brazoria County without notifying her.

Houston attorney S.C. Childress represented Gerald and Mildred Harris and said he was under no legal obligation to notify his fellow attorney about the custody hearing. He also dropped a figurative bombshell when he added that Clara told him during a meeting in October that she would follow David's intentions and place the boys with his lifelong friend, and executor of the estate, Dr. Robert Blanchard.

Then the grandparents notified the Galveston County Probate Court that they were being represented by another Houston lawyer, Barbara K. Twigg. She also represented their oldest son and uncle of the boys, 52-year-old Gerald Harris Jr.

Twigg asked Galveston County Probate Judge Gladys Burwell to name the uncle as guardian of the twins' financial interest in their father's estate, replacing Hoerster. The attorney told reporters that the uncle and the grandparents were in agreement and they were trying to work together and save money in legal expenses.

It will probably be years before all the collateral legal tangles and snarls left in the wake of the disaster are straightened out once and for all in the courts.

Working from prison through her defense attorneys, Clara hired Houston lawyer George "Mac" Secrest Jr. to spearhead her appeal. Secrest is one of the local legal community's leading experts in appellate law and was previously named as a special prosecutor to investigate reputed gag order violations in the case of another client of Parnham's, Andrea Yates. The former Harris County assistant district attorney also handled appeals for pickax killer Karla Faye Tucker.

One of Secrest's first tasks for Clara was expected to involve a close review of the thick transcript of her three-week trial to ferret out the most promising issues on which to base an appeal. With Clara's assets frozen, along with those of her deceased husband, as part of the court action filed on Lindsey's behalf, the imprisoned woman's supporters used e-mail in a campaign designed to raise $21,000 needed to pay for the transcripts.

During Clara's trial, Lindsey's mother amended the lawsuit seeking her former husband's estate for her daughter to include damage claims against Blue Moon Investigations and the Hilton Hotels Corp. Blue Moon operated under

SRSI Legal & Claims Services. The Hilton
corporation headquarters are in Beverly Hills,
California, but the Nassau Bay Hilton Inn was
owned by the New Clear Lake Hotel Limited
Partnership in Dallas.

By that time, Blue Moon Investigations had
entered into an agreement to cooperate with
CBS and film production agencies in a made-
for-TV movie and the suit asked for any
proceeds from sale of the Bachas' story rights
to be placed in a constructive trust controlled
by David's three children and ultimately to be
contributed to charity.

"Lindsey and the family want the money to be
turned over to children's victims charity in the
Harris County and Galveston area," attorney
Martin Webber explained. Webber was a member of the Davis & Davis law firm in Houston,
which represented Lindsey in the court action.

"The family's position is that they were not
going to sell the story and they don't think anybody should profit from the sale of the story,
particularly Blue Moon. Turning the money
over to a charity is one way to assure that
nobody profits from it."

The wrongful death lawsuit also asked for
monetary compensation from Blue Moon for
Lindsey and the twins. "Defendant Bobbi Bacha

even has the gall to propose the actors/actresses that should play the roles in the movie," it was declared in the court action.

Storyline Entertainment and Sony Pictures Television purchased an option on the story, arranged by the William Morris Agency. Blue Moon and the Bachas hired the high-powered talent management agency to market their story, according to the probate court filing.

CBS and Storyline Entertainment disclosed they were working on the film to be based on the extensive *Texas Monthly* articles by journalist Skip Hollandsworth. The story was said to be focused heavily on the role of the Bachas and Blue Moon Investigations.

Mrs. Shank, Lindsey's mother, continued to zero in on Blue Moon in the lawsuit for reputedly capitalizing on the notoriety of the case to publicize itself. She claimed the firm carried out a "publicity-hounding schedule of interviews regarding their involvement in the complex web of relationships surrounding the death of David L. Harris." A strong admonition against allowing the detective agency and the Bachas to "benefit from the death of David L. Harris — a death that defendant Blue Moon caused" was added by the protective parent.

Blue Moon was blamed in the action for

allegedly violating industry policy and its own policies by tipping Clara off to where her husband was. "You do not tell someone, your client, where someone is while they are with their paramour," the lawsuit said of the private detective agency. "These folks knew this ... and they violated their own policies and procedures."

Bobbi Bacha branded the lawsuit as frivolous and said of Clara: "I wish that she would have just stayed home with those babies that night. If she would have just been satisfied we were there, none of this would have happened. She could have taken him to the cleaners." It wasn't Blue Moon that was at fault, she insisted. It was Clara.

"Legally, if you hire us, we have to fulfill our contract and tell you what we know," she told a reporter. "Clara clearly breached our contract. She showed up to the scene of our investigation ... She drove the Mercedes. We didn't!"

Bobbi said she doubted she would ultimately realize more than $10,000 from the movie and cautioned that the lawsuit would force Blue Moon to file a breach of contract lawsuit against Clara and that could wind up costing Lindsey. "It's just going to come out of poor Lindsey's pot," Bobbi told reporters. "You can't keep someone from a public place. Clara certainly knew the hotel and gave us the address."

The private gumshoe then added an intriguing observation that seemed to clash strongly with Lindsey's recall of events immediately leading up to David's grisly death. "She was actually there stalking the parking lot an hour before we called," Bobbi said of her former client.

Clara had given up on locating her wandering husband and planned to call a halt to the search, but changed her plans when Lucas Bacha called on her cell phone, according to Lindsey. The woman, with her teenager riding in the passenger seat, then drove straight to the hotel.

"Such action was a clear violation of defendant Blue Moon's own policies and procedures and a clear departure from the standard of care exercised," it was claimed in the suit.

No amount was specified by the lawsuit in damages sought from Hilton, but it was claimed in the action that the hotel failed to train its employees in how to deal with domestic disputes, didn't notify police or detain the people involved until police arrived at the scene.

A spokeswoman for Hilton Hotels played it close to the vest when contacted by the press. She said it was company policy not to comment on pending litigation.

On Friday, Feb. 21, a week after sentencing,
Clara was officially taken into state custody and
transported from the Harris County Jail to the
Woodman Unit at Gatesville. At the prison she
was again fingerprinted and photographed
before being issued a standard prison uniform
of white trousers and shirt.

Then she was driven 135 miles northeast to a
state prison psychiatric facility just outside the
tiny community of Rusk in rural Cherokee
County a few miles north of Nacogdoches, where
a large amount of the debris from the doomed
space shuttle Columbia was recovered. The
Skyview Unit at Rusk accommodates prisoners
of both sexes, although not all inmates are under
psychiatric care. Clara was assigned to a single
cell and provided with an opportunity for
counseling while adjusting to life behind bars.

On Wednesday, March 19, she was given her
permanent prison assignment and driven
back to the Mountain View Prison at
Gatesville, about 40 miles west of Waco, to
serve the remainder of her sentence. She was
assigned to a dormitory-style housing unit
where most of the approximately 650 inmates
are doing their time. The relatively small number of inmates locked in more secure housing
at Mountain View include women held on the

female death row where Karla Tucker and Betty Beets spent their last years.

Dentists, doctors, lawyers and other professionals are not allowed to work in the jobs they were trained in, so the new inmate was put to work reconstructing old and damaged computers. It was a good assignment, as the other two primary work choices at Mountain View are in agriculture and livestock.

Clara and most of her fellow inmate "technicians" are required to get out of bed at 4 a.m. and put in 40-hour weeks working on the computers, which are donated to poor school districts after refurbishing. They do not have access to the Internet in the computer repair and maintenance shop. When she is not working, she is permitted to spend her time in a day room with 30 to 40 other inmates, watching television, reading, studying or writing letters.

Regardless of the stiff sentence Clara Harris received from a jury of her peers, a series of dramatically troubling events occurred shortly after the guilty verdict was returned in her sensational trial.

The weekend after Clara was sent to prison, a woman was accused of deliberately running her husband down with her Ford Taurus in the Liberty County Texas town of Hardin after flying into a rage because she thought he was cheating. The man was knocked into a muddy field and the driver was bringing her car around for another shot when a female clerk at a convenience store ran outside and placed herself between the victim and the speeding vehicle.

The courageous clerk said the driver swerved away at the last second, cursing and screaming. The injured man, who insisted he wasn't cheating on anybody, was treated at a hospital and released.

Early in March, another woman slashed her estranged husband with a knife, then ran down the fleeing man with her 1996 Ford Taurus in Webster after finding him walking in the parking lot of their apartment at 2:30 in the morning with a female friend. He was taken by ambulance to Memorial Hermann Hospital with a broken leg and his spouse surrendered to Harris County law enforcement authorities a few hours later.

Despite the jury's conviction and sentencing of Clara Harris, it appeared that the "Murder by Mercedes" had led at least a few spurned wives to declare open season on husbands suspected of straying.

Such acts of obvious emulation by strangers were not the only reward Clara Harris received as she began to serve out her 20-year prison sentence for running over her husband in a jealous rage. Galveston County Probate Judge Gladys Burwell granted close to $1.2 million in assets out of the large estate left by David Harris' murder to be retained by Clara, while each of his three children will be entitled to roughly $2 million.

"If it were not for her, it would not be an issue," Gerald Harris said during a three-hour hearing, making an abrupt about-face from his compassionate support of his daughter-in-law during the trial. He added to the *Houston Chronicle*, "She was the cause of my son's death."

Under the terms of the settlement, Lindsey Harris will receive $1.756 million, as will her 4-year-old twin half-brothers, Brian and Bradley Harris. Under the agreement, Clara was left with the Friendswood home, appraised at more than $700,000, a home in Lake Livingston valued at $130,000 and $160,000 in a retirement account.

Gerald Harris said he did not believe the settlement was "fair and reasonable ... Clara is receiving more than she has a right to."

The same man who professed "love" and "Christian compassion" now decided to draw the line when it came to money, proving everyone has their breaking point.